The Good Soldier

From Austrian Social Democracy to Communist
Captivity with a Soldier of Panzer-Grenadier Division
"Grossdeutschland"

Alfred Novotny

THE ABERJONA PRESS
Bedford, Pennsylvania

To Eva, with Love

All photos and graphics, except as noted, are from the author's private collection.

Chapter Introductions: Marc Rikmenspoel
Technical Editors: Marc Rikmenspoel and Keith E. Bonn
Production: Patricia K. Bonn
Printer: Automated Graphic Systems

The Aberjona Press is an imprint of Aegis Consulting Group, Inc.,
        Bedford, Pennsylvania 15522
© 2003 Alfred Novotny
Printed in the United States of America
10 09 08 07 06 05 04   6 5 4 3 2

ISBN: 0-9666389-9-9

Contents

Acknowledgments

The author wishes to express his sincere appreciation to the following individuals who, among others, helped to make this book:

My good friend, Jerry Klein, for encouraging me to write this book and for his friendship and invaluable input at my first edition.

Marc Rikmenspoel for his great knowledge of WWII and Division *"Grossdeutschland"* in particular, his excellent writing skills, and concern for authenticity

Keith E. Bonn, editor and publisher, for his great subject knowledge and unending help.

Mark Burdess for is assistance in graphic matters and his loyalty.

William Wilsen, Ph.D., for his picture contribution of Vienna. It meant a lot to me.

And, above all, Lisl, my good wife and companion for over fifty years, for her patience and understanding during my long hours of writing this book.

Rank Equivalences

US Army	Soviet Army	German Army	Waffen-SS
General of the Army	Marshal Sovetskogo Soyuza	Generalfeldmarschall	
General	General Armiyi	Generaloberst	SS-Oberstgruppenführer
Lieutenant General	General Polkovnik	General (der Infanterie, der Artillerie, etc.)	SS-Obergruppenführer
Major General	General Leytenant	Generalleutnant	SS-Gruppenführer
Brigadier General	General Major	Generalmajor	SS-Brigadeführer
			SS-Oberführer
Colonel	Polkovnik	Oberst	SS-Standartenführer
Lieutenant Colonel	Podpolkovnik	Oberstleutnant	SS-Obersturmbannführer
Major	Major	Major	SS-Sturmbannführer
Captain	Kapetan	Hauptmann	SS-Hauptsturmführer
1st Lieutenant	Starshiy Leytenant	Oberleutnant	SS-Obersturmführer
	Leytenant		
2nd Lieutenant	Mladshiy Leytenant	Leutnant	SS-Untersturmführer
Sergeant Major*		Stabsfeldwebel	SS-Sturmscharführer
Master Sergeant/ First Sergeant	Starshina	Oberfeldwebel	SS-Hauptscharführer
Technical Sergeant	Starshiy Serzhant	Feldwebel	SS-Oberscharführer
Staff Sergeant		Unterfeldwebel	SS-Scharführer
Sergeant	Serzhant	Unteroffizier	SS-Unterscharführer
Corporal	Mladshiy Serzhant		
Private First Class	Yefreytor	Hauptgefreiter Obergefreiter Gefreiter	SS-Rottenführer
		Obersoldat (Obergrenadier, Oberkanonier, etc.)	SS-Sturmmann
Private	Krasnoarmeyets	Soldat (Grenadier, Kanonier, etc.)	SS-Mann

*Not a rank in the US Army during WWII. NCOs serving as sergeants major during that era were usually Master Sergeants.

Introduction

What you are about to read is the second version of Alfred "Fred" Novotny's memoirs. The original edition, self-published during 1996, was written mainly for family and friends, and avoided some of the more unpleasant events of the author's wartime experience. Now he has decided to share the story of his life in full detail. The awful incidents concomitant to life on the Eastern Front during World War II and in the post-war Soviet prison camp system are laid bare, as a warning and example for future generations.

Fred Novotny was born in Vienna on 1 April 1924; thus, he was perfectly placed to suffer the ancient Chinese curse: "May you live in interesting times." His times were interesting and deadly, but that he survived them is not the greatest surprise. Rather, what stands out is that Fred never lost his compassion, nor his humanity, nor his mind.

It must be stated now that this is not an account that caters to the "adreneline junkie." There are other books filled with sensational accounts of frontline combat, often told without any sense of loss or consequence. A reader might almost imagine that time did not exist before or after the war. Novotny's memoir is something different; it is the story of an era as much as the story of a man. It is the story of Europe and of America during the twentieth century, of how one man fared while caught in the vice of history. We are left with an example of how to retain all the best within ourselves, and with the hope that we could live with matching dignity, should we find ourselves living in interesting times.

Fred Novotny remembers . . .

May 1945. How could this be happening? I asked myself this question for the hundredth time. Here the war was over and soldiers were supposed to go home when the war ended, were they not? I had been so close to home, a few miles from my parents' place in Vienna. It would have been so easy to lay aside my rifle and become a deserter as thousands of others had, and just walk home.

But I hadn't. I was a good soldier. Now here I was, dragging those last few hideously painful steps on our agonizing march—a veritable hunger march in which many died—into the Caucasus Mountains to the Soviet prison camp at Tkvibuli.

It looked almost nondescript, just like any other camp. A series of barracks were arranged like steps up the hillside. Barbed wire and guard towers were everywhere. Treeless hills surrounded the camp, as inhospitable as a moonscape. This was to be our home, our place of punishment. But for how long?

First, as the *Wehrmacht* began its massive collapse in the spring of 1945, we had been captured by the Americans. That had been a good sign. It portended a quick release and subsequent freedom. Then the Russians arrived and, suddenly, we were their prisoners. We had fought them and they claimed the right to take us. We were herded at last onto a train, as awful as anything that can be imagined, rolling endless miles on a journey I would like to forget, but can't.

Now there is this infernal camp.

Already it is cold at night. We are broken men. We have lost the war and now we are targets for revenge by the Russians whose hatred for us is unyielding and uncompromising. They will not forget what we have done to their country, their army, their people.

So begins my time, my share of that revenge at the camp which most people have never heard of, and where we are destined to become forgotten men . . . and many of us dead men.

1

Peace, Poverty, and Social Democracy

Vienna, 1928

It will be difficult for many readers, particularly Americans of post-war generations, to comprehend the living conditions of Novotny's childhood. He grew up during the beginning of the last phase of the Industrial Revolution, a time when technological advances were making life easier for the citizens of industrialized nations, but when those luxuries were mostly unavailable to the majority of citizens. The Great Depression worsened living conditions, and helped to create the situation in which Adolf Hitler and National Socialism seemed to offer the best future for Germany and for Austria.

Fred Novotny remembers . . .

I remember the small room filled with much chatter and laughter. I was only four years old and there are a great many things I do not remember. I did not understand the things people were saying to one another. There were bottles of wine on a long table. The smell of *Schnitzel* being fried reached my bed, which I shared with my sister, Jutta. It was the celebration of my mother's wedding—her second. My father had died when I was very young, only two. I do not remember him at all.

The *Wohnung,* or flat, was small and cramped, but I found out later we had far better accommodations than most people in Vienna at that time. There was a walkway from the kitchen out to a long concrete balcony. More importantly, the apartment had a water closet with a toilet, and few people had such luxuries. We had running water—cold only—and there was a bedroom large enough for just two beds. Mama and Papa had their bed, and there was one for my sister, Jutta, and me. We had a dining room table, four chairs, and a large wardrobe with a wood-cased radio on top. There was a basket under the kitchen table for a few of our toys. The window overlooked the balcony, but it was still quite dark, for we lived on the second floor and the building across the street was four stories high, and it blocked out all sunlight.

This was part of a new housing complex built by the Socialist government and named after August Bebel, a Socialist leader. The three hundred apartments of the *Bebelhof*

Four great women (L–R): Lisl's mother; my wife, Lisl; my Mama; our daughter, Eva. Taken on a visit home to Vienna, 1960.

were all occupied by workers with sympathies or loyalties to the Social Democratic Party. Even at this early age, our lives were significantly influenced by politics.

The whole building was a huge square with entrances on all sides. The main entrance was guarded by a big iron gate and everything was very secure. Each block of twelve apartments had its own *Stiegenhaus,* or entrance stairway, and one community laundry room, the *Waschküche.* This was in the basement along with a small coal cellar. The room used to dry the clothes was four stories up, under the roof, with no elevator access. Each family was allowed one workday in the laundry per month, and it was very hard work for the mothers. The men would never do this kind of work.

Inside the huge square of the complex was a wading pool, with a six-foot bronze fish head gushing water. There were benches for mothers to sit and watch their children and a playground, and walkways on which to run. Playing in the grass and bushes was forbidden and there were typical Austrian signs, *"das betreten des Grasses ist Verboten"* ("Walking on the grass is forbidden"). Still it was a paradise for children. We were not allowed to leave the *Hof,* or square, without the consent of our parents. They felt safe leaving us unsupervised to play in the *Hof.*

Vienna, 1928. Novotny, his sister, Jutta, and his "Mama."

The apartment also had a small room, called a *Kabinet*, where *Grossvater* (grandfather) lived. This was my new father's father, a retired cabinetmaker. He had been born in Czechoslovakia and had a very strong accent; he also liked his rum several times a day. He seldom left his room, or so it seemed to us. My sister and I visited him on occasion and would sit on his small bed while he told us stories. The room smelled strongly of rum and Mama was not too happy when we went to see him.

Life in general, however, seemed wonderful to us. In the summertime, we spent much of the day around the wading pool. Once a week, the gardeners worked about the *Hof* and they sometimes would playfully spray us with their garden hoses. In the winter, we would build snowmen and have snowball fights. The older kids would pour buckets of water on the pavement so we could run and slide, much to the dismay of the adults.

My new father was a gentle man with a friendly smile and a kind face. He was very strong because of the heavy work he had to do. He drove a milk truck for a large dairy. Trucks were not refrigerated back then, but he kept the milk and butter cold with large chunks of ice he carried. He left the apartment every day except Sunday at 4:00 A.M. I even remember him before I was four, when he visited at *Oma's* (Grandma's) where we lived before Mama got remarried.

Oma's was a very small apartment on the fourth floor (fifth by American reckoning, since we called the ground floor the *Erdgeschoss*, and the floor above it, the "first floor"). There were no elevators, of course. Here my mother lived with her mother, my baby sister, and me. The place had a very small kitchen with a stove, one small table jammed against the wall, and two chairs. There also was a room with two single beds, one for *Oma* and Mama and one for Jutta and me.

Mama's new husband-to-be would sometimes let me ride on his back. He would get down on all fours, like a horse, and now and then he would buck and I would fly what seemed very high up. I laughed a lot and I remember that until this day.

The best Papa and his son, Fredy in Vienna, 1928. I was then four, and he about twenty-eight.

These are the earliest days I can remember, and on one of them, while *Oma*, Mama, and her husband-to-be were talking, I disappeared under the table and soon came out screaming wildly. I had peeled and eaten two whole cloves of garlic and nobody wanted to come near me for the next two days. The smell was too much.

Jutta, who was two and a half years my junior, and I were afraid to sleep alone at *Oma's* because she had a huge parrot she brought from Argentina, where part of her family had settled. When she wanted us to be peaceful and quiet, she would tell us the bird was watching and could talk and tell her if we misbehaved. We believed her. I also remember a shiny brass samovar brought home by *Opa* (grandfather) on one of his trips to southwestern Russia. He was a representative of an Austrian perfume company, and Europe and Russia were part of his territory. He died at the young age of forty-two and, as it turned out, I was many years later to find myself in many of the Russian cities my grandfather knew so well. I also remember that *Oma* had a very lifelike, meter-high inflatable white stork, which was scary for me and Jutta. He would stand in the bedroom on his spindly red legs, moving constantly in the slightest breeze. Even though he was made of rubber, I would stick my head under the comforter, afraid to look at him, sometimes sweating in fear all night long.

In the years before the annexation of Austria by Germany, Vienna was run by the Social Democrats and was very strongly labor-oriented. On Sundays, families would gather with their children. The men and boys wore French blue shirts and held up red flags with three arrows in the corner, which was the symbol of "forward-moving" Socialism and a better world for the working class tomorrow . . . or so we were told.

The Social Democrats, mostly blue-collar workers and intellectuals, were strongly opposed to Soviet-style Communism, almost as much as they were opposed to German National Socialism. The Vienna *Gemeinde Rat* (city council) was made up completely of Social Democrats, and pushed to build better housing for workers. In a six-year span, more than two hundred dwellings such as our own *Bebelhof* were built. Workers with Social Democrat affiliations got special treatment and the lucky families, of which we were one, moved into the new buildings.

This arrangement allowed thousands of families to have running cold water and toilets for the first time. Even though these apartments were small by today's standards, they were clean and dry, with that long balcony accessible from the kitchen. They were a startling contrast to the ancient buildings (hundreds of years old!) known as *"Feuchte Wohnungen"* (damp flats) which everyone knew so well, which had no indoor plumbing at all. How Mama must have loved the new place. I remember her painting walls, seemingly all the time. A man in Europe at that time would never do such work at home.

I also remember Mama playing the violin. She was about twenty-five or twenty-six at the time. We really never knew how good she was or could have become at the instrument, but she loved it.

Life was good in those years. Papa had a steady job. The year 1929 brought a second sister to our family named Gusti. She was a beautiful child with dark eyes and dark hair and she grew up to have a great sense of humor.

Then Papa bought Mama a truly outrageous gift, the first electric sewing machine available in the city. It cost 600 Austrian schillings and Papa made but 50 schillings a week.

Fred Novotny drawing of St. Stephens Cathedral in Vienna while a prisoner at Camp Georgia, Russia, 1946. Done from memory.

Novotny's sister, Gusti,
1949.

He bought it American style—*auf Schulden* (on credit)—and
this was very unusual anywhere in Europe at the time, when
people saved from January to September to buy fall clothes,
and from September to May to buy spring clothes.

Mama made drapes for the apartment with her new
sewing machine, and something called *Kleiderschürzen*,
which were work aprons worn over the dress at home to protect it. In those days, women did not own many dresses.

At the peak of the Depression in 1930, everyone in Austria
was hit very hard, just as the many were in the rest of the
world. Papa's job was on the line. It was a day-to-day strug-
gle and I often heard my parents discussing what to give us
to eat and how to keep us clothed.

This was the time I first heard the famous Viennese
expression, *Tante Dorothea* (Aunt Dorothy), a nickname for
the Vienna *Versatzamt*. This was a municipally-owned pawn
shop, as big as Marshall Field's in Chicago and with branch-
es in every district of the city. *Tante Dorothea* was the place
common working people went to pawn things to keep their
heads above water, that is, to feed their families, pay the rent,
and pay the utility bills. There was no money for other
expenses. Everything went for food and shelter.

In the spring, all the family winter clothes and anything
not nailed down (including Mama's new sewing machine)
went to the pawn shop. The process was reversed in the fall,

when Papa's bike and things like the radio and wedding rings had to go until they could be retrieved again. This was not always possible. Families would fall behind more and more, bringing the things they bought for a good price to *Tante Dorothea* where they got very little for them and could not always retrieve them. Everybody was involved, but people were still embarrassed to be seen there. Sometimes families would send their children to the pawn shop, not realizing how ashamed and embarrassed we felt. Such was life.

Vienna, 1934

Hitler's seizure of power as German Chancellor in early 1933 had a dramatic impact on Austrian political and economic fortune. Amid growing political agitation, in March, the Christian Socialist Chancellor Dollfuss suspended the Austrian parliament; invoking a 1917 law giving the government special powers in an emergency situation, he prohibited political assemblies or rallies, and limited freedom of the press. By May, wearing political uniforms was forbidden, and the Austrian Communist Party and National Socialist (Nazi) Party were both outlawed. These measures only aggravated the already incendiary situation, and both parties continued to exist on a clandestine basis.

Intended as a unifying measure, Dollfuss formed the Fatherland Front (Vaterländische Front) in an attempt to rally broad-based support for Austrian nationalism. This nationalistic vision also included unity based on the pervasive influence of the Roman Catholic Church across Austria. By early 1934, however, it was obvious that this solution was not acceptable to all factions. In February, a police search for weapons in Linz triggered a general strike by Socialist labor, and significant fighting in Vienna.

After four days, the Socialist rebellion was quelled, and the Social Democrat Party, along with affiliated trade unions, was outlawed; the Fatherland Front remained the only legal political entity in Austria. Although four years of relative tranquility resulted, the underground political activity proliferated, and the day of reckoning was only postponed.

Fred Novotny remembers . . .

By 1934, unemployment had become intolerable and unrest among the workers grew stronger and more threatening. The government at the time was under the rule of the *Schwarzen* (the "blacks," or Christian Socialists)—so-called by the workers because it consisted largely of the politically strong, black-clad Catholic clergy and an army of government bureaucrats called *Beamte.* This was a title widely sought since it meant security for life, perhaps with low pay, but with no hard work and a workday that ended at 4:00 P.M. It included anyone working for the phone system, the railroad, the postal service, the police and fire departments, and any other government office. Those who worked in these departments were immensely secure. As unrest grew, the government strengthened its grip.

The police forces were beefed up with army troops called the *Heimwehr,* or home guard. One day in February 1934, when I was about ten, I was listening to our crystal set (the box radio had been taken to the pawnshop) and there were words I did not understand coming across the airwaves, such as *Standrecht,* or martial law, and *Ausgehverbot,* or curfew. In Vienna, our world was about to grow ugly.

We were waiting for Papa to come home on that 10th of February and we were worried because we knew his work would keep him out after the 6:00 P.M. curfew. On this day, he did not come home and we were terribly frightened. During the night, Mama tried to comfort us by saying that everything would be all right. The next morning, I heard her crying in the kitchen and there was another long day of worrying about Papa's whereabouts.

Then, finally, at 6:00 P.M. on 11 February, Papa slowly walked in through the door. He tried to look cheerful but we knew something was wrong. As he slowly removed his work clothes, Mama nearly fainted. His body was a bloody mess— there were heavy welts, and long black and blue streaks across his back and arms. Nevertheless, he was alive.

As we feared, Papa had been arrested on 10 February after 6:00 P.M. The authorities would not let him explain why he was on the street at that time. They did not believe what he tried to tell them; namely, that he could not help being on the street after the curfew because it was his job, and that he had gotten behind in his deliveries by running into the many barricades that had sprung up all over Vienna that day.

So he was put in the police wagon and taken to the station and beaten throughout the night. Finally, he was released after his company tried to locate him and his truck. Afterward, he was understandably bitter. He swore to fight this kind of government the rest of his life. Even now, I can see my father with that blood-encrusted body, and I remember that frightening night when he did not come home.

By 12 February, the civil war had erupted. By 6:00 A.M., women were spreading the word that the police were conducting a house-to-house search for weapons. Overnight, the apartment complexes of the workers had become fortresses. Many workers were suspected of hiding guns, and with the aid of the strong Social Democrat Party of Czechoslovakia, workers indeed did have guns and were occupying the roofs and dormer windows of their buildings, trying to prevent house searches.

For two days, rifle and pistol shots could be heard all around Vienna. On the third day, the staccato pounding of heavy machine-gun fire erupted as the workers sought to defend their buildings. There were stories of heavy fighting in other parts of the city, of heroic battles with workers holding their buildings against all odds.

We lived on the first floor and suddenly we felt an immense vibration coming from the street below. Mama peeked through the window and shouted, *"Panzer!"* (tanks). She chased us into the furthest corner of the apartment and pushed two big wardrobes in front of the windows. After about half an hour, the armored vehicles opened fire with machine guns and cannon. We heard our wardrobe barricades get hit several times. Mama was lying on top of us to shield us. We did not understand what was going on, but we were scared stiff.

The shelling and shooting went on into 15 February and then, suddenly, it was totally quiet. The civil war had stopped. Thousands of Social Democrats were arrested and sent to concentration camps. Hundreds of workers and members of their families had died. The Social Democrat leaders fled to Czechoslovakia and the red-white-red flag of Austria replaced the red flag with three arrows all over Vienna. It was February 1934, and the way had been paved for Hitler.

The Nazis first attempted to seize power in Vienna in the summer of 1934 and it was a fiasco. They killed Chancellor Dollfuss and managed to occupy the government building at the Ballhausplatz, but they did not intervene in Austrian affairs directly. The country's "Fatherland Front" grew strong again, and Austria seemed under the firm control of a new chancellor, Dr. Kurt Schuschnigg. The government was guaranteed by the governments of England, France, and Italy—all of which proved to be paper tigers as history would show. Naturally, all this was beyond the comprehension of a ten-year-old boy.

Vienna, 1938

Again, it will likely be difficult for many American readers to comprehend Novotny's life, entering the work force at the age of fourteen to begin a predetermined career. Today, the choice of a career is taken for granted, and the following will show why this privilege should be cherished by those who possess it.

Fred Novotny remembers . . .

As the son of an active and dedicated Social Democrat, I grew up in an atmosphere in which workers' rights, and achieving them, were most important to my father. Along with other workers' families, we would gather at the *"Wiese"* (glen), a sort of picnic area without benches or shelters.

Fathers and sons would mostly play soccer or sit and talk about politics. The *Schwarzen* were always more afraid of the Socialists and the "Reds" than they were of the National Socialists (the *"Nazis,"* so called because of the German pronunciation of the first word in the party title). We boys had worn French blue shirts with the red insignia with three arrows.

As per my father, Social Democrats were anti-National Socialism, anti-Communism, and anti-Fatherland Front. The resolution of the uprising described earlier settled all these questions.

School had ended and under different circumstances and in better times, I would have had a good chance to go into a *Gymnasium* (college preparatory school) and, as my father said, become more in life than he ever could. When he was fourteen in 1914, Papa lived in the 12th District, a typical workingman's area, with his twelve brothers and sisters. The street was called the *Ruckergasse* and I still go there on my trips home to stand in front of the building and contemplate his life and times. The family was extremely poor. His father had been an out-of-work carpenter. So my father, at age fourteen, was first to help support the family. He had to quit school and take on such jobs as mopping hospital floors, carrying sacks of coal and the like, all for a loaf of bread. That was a feast for the family, especially during the dark years of World War I.

He was drafted in 1917, when things were not going well for Austria-Hungary. Instead of fighting where most of the Imperial and Royal Army was committed, in Italy or on the Eastern Front, he ended up being assigned to a unit fighting in France. Fortunately for all of us, he came through his brief combat experience unscathed. After the war ended in 1918, he returned home and resumed his role as the family's sole breadwinner.

In 1938, the depression still affected us, as it did much of the world. Papa had a job, which produced very little money, but we always had food, even though it was very simple. We had meat only once a week, and then, about two ounces.

One day my father said to me, "*Bua* (which is dialect for "boy"), let's go and find you a place to work." He said I should be in a position where I would never have to be hungry, like that of a *Zuckerbäcker* (pastry cook) or in a hotel or restaurant as a cook or waiter. He said they would give me room and board and I would learn a trade.

Since he drove a dairy truck and delivered to restaurants, coffeehouses, and hotels, he had some connections. So Papa told me to get dressed and Mama gave me a clean shirt. I had shined my shoes the night before and Mama made sure my nails were clean and my hair combed.

Papa took my hand and we went to several places to see "important people" who might give me the opportunity to become a *Lehrling* (apprentice). I think Mama cried because I was so young and would have to leave our home for three years. I remember how overwhelmed I was when, for the first time in my life, I saw huge, luxurious rooms with glittering chandeliers, velvet-covered walls, Persian carpets, and well-dressed employees scurrying about busily. I was so scared I couldn't imagine I would ever learn to fit in such places or even understand what they wanted.

Then, there I was, starting as a *Kellener Und Koch Lehrling* (a cook's and waiter's apprentice) at the famous Kahlenberg Restaurant in Vienna. It was 1 July 1938. The Kahlenberg at that time was the largest food operation in Austria, seating more than 3,000 patrons at a time. It had many dining rooms, as well as open terraces and gardens, and one could easily get lost. It was owned by *Gemeinde Wien*, the municipality of

Some of the crew of the Kahlenberg Restaurant pose to commemorate the first day on the job for apprentice waiter Fred Novotny, 1 July 1938. Novotny is receiving a literal "bear hug."

Vienna, and was managed by the firm of Kröger and Lob, two men from an old hotel family.

The younger man was Director Max Lob, a fireball of a manager who was wholly business-minded and who demanded hard work. Nevertheless, he was compassionate and friendly. His partner, *Herr* Director Kröger was a Chicago-born Austrian with the air of an aristocrat, and his job was strictly public relations. He was not often seen working, but spent his time in the various dining rooms watching the waiters and the guests.

I remember that one month after I started, on 1 August, I got my first paycheck. It came to ten Austrian schillings, about fifty cents in American currency. I bought a white shirt and a black tie and I proudly took the remaining five schillings to Mama and Papa. What a thrill.

My parents also were proud of me since I lived and worked in such fine, rich surroundings. They constantly encouraged me. Every month from then on, I contributed a small sum from my paycheck to my parents. They never asked, but I felt I owed it to them and I am glad I could give them something.

My job benefits included a room I shared with three other apprentices. It was clean and comfortable, but hardly lavish. There were four beds and a coal stove. Because so many employees worked late and because the buses stopped running at midnight, the restaurant was compelled to provide housing for many of its employees, especially as it was located on a mountain outside of Vienna.

We worked ten hours a day, sometimes longer, six days a week. One of the days was a school day at the hotel and restaurant school. We studied gastronomy, cooking, the art of waiting on tables, French and English, history, biology, and the like. I learned fast and found the profession chosen for me to be truly satisfying.

In 1940, I was told by the owner at the restaurant that I was the best apprentice they had; I was good in school and proud to learn that what I did was appreciated. More and more guests asked for me personally when they had special wishes. I adopted the philosophy that nothing less than one hundred percent would be good enough.

2

National Socialism and War

Changing Attitudes

*Life changed for Fred's family with the shifting politics between
1934 and 1941. The 1938 "Anschluss," or "annexation" of
Austria was effected by a* de facto *occupation of the Austrian state
by the armed forces of Germany. To that point, it was difficult to
argue against Hitler, since living conditions improved in many
ways, and the German Army was at first resurgent, then consistently victorious. It was during this time that the Austrians
became "Germans," citizens of the* Grossdeutsche *(Greater
German)* Reich. *Austria, once the* Österreich, *or Eastern Empire,
was now a province known as the* Ostmark, *the East Borderland.*

Fred Novotny remembers . . .

When the armed forces of Nazi Germany occupied Austria,
my indoctrination changed and so did I. By age seventeen, I
was convinced that Hitler, and Hitler only, was the answer to
our woes.

I was never required to serve in the German Youth or the
Hitler Youth, and I was never threatened with any sort of ret-
ribution for not going along with the crowd. The closest I
ever came to participation in Party events were several occasions just after the *Anschluss* when my friends at the restaurant and I were handed black corduroy shorts, belts, shirts,
and armbands, and were told to attend rallies in the
Heldenplatz in front of government buildings. At fourteen,

18

one does not comprehend the meaning of such artificial, phony ceremonies. I simply read the papers and listened to the radio, which all carried the Nazi Party line, and listened to my superiors at work and in the hotel school. In those days, there were very few radio stations that could transmit beyond their local areas, and I did not understand any language but German in any case. The words from the *Volksempfänger* (an inexpensive radio that the Nazis encouraged every family to own) were consistent and completely beguiling. Quite simply, I was overwhelmed by what seemed to be the clear, straightforward messages being delivered by every medium, at home and at work.

At work, a waiter, Mr. Reimer, was appointed as the Nazi Party functionary in our restaurant. Even at this low level, the Party carefully ensured its presence. The net result was that I bought into the basic concepts of the Party— Germany's destiny, Hitler's genius, and so on. I just did not know better, despite Papa's convictions to the contrary.

Gradually, it became apparent that Papa and I no longer saw eye to eye. We argued over political issues, and with the certainty of youth, I was absolutely sure he no longer understood the world . . . even though he was barely forty years old. Papa always would say, "Hitler will destroy the world. Fredy, if you survive the war, you will understand what I am saying now. Germany can never win a war against the Allies; look at the World War."

I do remember these words now, and I have understood him well since 1945.

The Salami Caper

After World War II began during September 1939, Hitler and the German government were determined to avoid conditions of civilian suffering that might cause civil unrest, such as had plagued the war effort in both Germany and Austria-Hungary during the Great War. Therefore, in many ways, including for Novotny, life continued as it had before the war. The obvious exception to this was that persecution of Jews was suddenly open and legal.

Fred Novotny remembers . . .

Life at the Kahlenberg was certainly not all work and no play. We were still kids and, like all kids, we played our share of pranks.

There was, for instance, our chef, *Herr* Steinbichler. He seemed to be a harsh man. He was extremely handsome with a proud, black mustache and a powerful, athletic build. He had a particular weakness, and that was his love for Hungarian salami, which was very expensive, very rare, and is still today the best in the world. Every day, he would slice off a piece at around 10:00 in the morning, order a *Viertel* (a glass of Viennese new wine) and sit down to enjoy the good life.

We apprentices watched this procedure every day and wanted to taste the salami he so enjoyed. He kept it in a walk-in cooler made of redwood. He hung the salami on a short string from a nail in the wall. So obsessed was he that no one else should share his precious salami that he would mark the spot where he had cut off the last piece. Upon his arrival, he would check carefully to see that no one had eaten any of his salami.

One day, we four apprentices were scheming how we could all taste this forbidden delicacy. I came up with the idea that we use a longer string matching the one on top of the salami, and then cut off a piece of salami and extend the string. That way the line would always be the same as the mark he made the day before.

The salami was great. We were laughing because we were so clever, but we didn't know when to quit. For three days, the string got longer and longer and the salami shorter and shorter. In fact, it became so short that the chef finally noticed, and with a voice like a bear, he cried out, "Alfred, Karl, Franz, Erich, down to the walk-in on the double." We dutifully arrived at the cooler. The chef did not say a word. His black eyes were sparkling. He simply pointed at the salami, then slapped each of us in the face, left and right. No questions were asked.

Then he pronounced sentence. I received three weeks in the potato cellar. Karl was given three weeks washing pots and pans, Franz was awarded three weeks of carrot peeling, and Erich got three weeks of window washing. This occupied three hours before even beginning our daily work. It was hard, but every time we saw one another, we would break out in laughter over our clever prank. Later, we found out that the chef had told a friend about our ingenious idea and even he laughed.

The Strudel Caper

We were always hungry, even with three square meals a day. The temptations were plentiful. The bakery was in the basement of our huge restaurant, and it produced the most wonderful pastries, tortes, strudels, and breads. We were tormented by the proximity of all those tasty morsels day after day. There was a dumbwaiter serving three kitchens, one on the lower floor where the pastry shop and storeroom were located, another on the main floor where the restaurant was located, and the other on the upper floor with its banquet kitchen.

One day, we finally got Karl to help the pastry chef. The chef, as Karl discovered, would go to the main kitchen for lunch at 1:30 P.M. daily. Karl told Erich and me to be there at 1:30, at which time he would load the dumbwaiter with pastries and we would pull it up to the upper floor where we all had a date to fill our stomachs.

Unfortunately, our eyes were bigger than our stomachs. So much was loaded on the dumbwaiter that no matter how we tried we could not eat it all. We left the rest on the dumbwaiter and I felt so full and nauseated I could scarcely move. We had each eaten six to eight pieces of rich, creamy pastries.

Despite punishment, a virtual repeat of the previous month, many small and large pranks followed. Two of them still stick out in my mind.

Black coffee, or mocha, was outrageously expensive. At that time it was five schillings a cup with no refills. For five schillings you could eat a pork roast or a schnitzel. Even today, coffee in Austria is priced out of proportion. Nowhere in Europe could an employee avail himself of a free cup of coffee, as in the United States.

Our headwaiter, Mr. Utner, loved his mocha in large cups, double-mocha. He made good money, so every day he would buy himself a cup. Often the waiters would call him to attend to a guest and some employee would take a sip of his precious coffee. To counter this practice, Mr. Utner wrote a note one day and put it by his cup. It read, "Do not touch: I spit in it." He then found another note which said, "Me, too." So much for protecting the precious mocha.

On another occasion, when I was maybe sixteen and still a waiter's apprentice (becoming a qualified waiter in Europe takes about three years), I saw the waiters go by a table and coming back laughing and talking and repeating their trip. I became very curious and asked one of the waiters what was causing such interest.

"You must see this," he told me. Not to be overly obvious, I took a small silver tray with two glasses of water since it was one of the apprentices' jobs to change glasses often and see that fresh water was on the tables. As I approached this particular table, it was immediately clear what caused such interest. At the table was a man with a lady of about thirty who had a dress cut so low it showed off her two beautiful, large breasts. She turned to me, quietly, and smiled, knowing why I was there. Blood rushed into my cheeks as I looked at her special attractions. I slowly put the tray down, my eyes fastened on her. But the tray was not on the table, but in her lap. I froze. I was so embarrassed I could not think. Seconds later I was on my knees on the floor, wiping her lap, her crotch area, nonstop. Everyone broke up laughing. The head-waiter sent me back to my punishment in the potato cellar.

Between learning my trade and these occasional pranks, life for me as a young apprentice waiter in the new *"Ostmark"* went on largely as it had before the Nazi takeover. I suppose it was so for most Austrians. For others, however, it was a different story. Danger was thrust upon some, while others chose to accept it. My uncle was one of the former, and

Mama was one of the latter; she faced dangers and made sacrifices that were as unusual as they were courageous.

Even when we were children, she had this desire to help anybody, man or animal, and she often came home from the market telling us about the poor cat or dog left by some people and how she bought some sausage to feed the poor creatures. On occasion, she would bring home an animal that actually belonged to some one else, and the owners would run all over looking for their pets.

Mama's only sister, Mimi, had married a Jew, whom we knew as Uncle Otto. He was an engineer and they had two children, Ossi and Edith, approximately the same ages as my sister, Jutta, and me. It was 1939 and the Nazis had been in control in Austria for over a year. Most Jews had either been rounded up or had left the country, but not Uncle Otto. He said he was born in Vienna, was married to an Aryan, and had nothing to fear.

One day, the SA (*die Sturmabteilungen*, or "Storm Troopers," the official name for the Nazi Brownshirts) were coming to pick him up. He happened to be away from home. Mimi told Mama and she went looking for him to warn him. She found him and brought him into our very small home at night and told him she was going to hide him until he could leave Austria with his family. This was very dangerous. Our next-door neighbor, *Herr* Bene, was a high-ranking Nazi. Even though we had a good relationship as neighbors, he could not find out.

Until the *Anschluss*, *Herr* Bene was a quiet and friendly neighbor whose political affiliations were unknown to us. After the Nazi takeover, he suddenly became both a Nazi Party official and a prosperous owner of a printing business. How his situation so rapidly improved, we didn't know. Perhaps he was awarded deed to a business confiscated from Jews; in any event, he lost everything—power, prestige, money—after the war ended.

Nevertheless, at the time, we had to make sure he did not find out about Uncle Otto. We had a little anteroom before the kitchen. Mother hung a portrait of Hitler opposite our entrance, always turned around, unless someone rang the doorbell. Then she would turn it back so it appeared this was a good Aryan family.

It was terrible. We could only whisper with Otto and never say his name. His family could not come close to our apartment. Otto always was worried to death we children would make a mistake and say something at the playground or at school. So our family's wellbeing was endangered since the penalty for hiding a Jew was a concentration camp for the family, or worse.

After a few weeks, Aunt Mimi was able to get her children, Ossi and Edith, to be taken to Switzerland, and from there to England. It was very hard for parents and children to separate in this way, but there was no choice. Then one morning, Otto was gone and we learned later they were all in England. We were immensely relieved not to have this constant danger any longer. They were safe.

After the war, I found out that Mama had a job at the Red Cross as a nursing assistant and would be sent to the railroad station to give coffee and food to soldiers, wounded or otherwise. Rolling through Vienna, she knew, there were many POW transports carrying Russians, French, British, and others. Mother was up to living dangerously again. She would acquire and hoard food, waiting for the POW transports, talking her way through by saying she was ordered by the head of the Red Cross to feed the prisoners.

She was happiest when she could say, "I gave this to two young French or Russian prisoners of war." She simply helped and never thought of the consequences. She could have been caught and dealt with harshly, but she was lucky. She was one of the unsung heroes of the war, unrecognized, but unselfishly doing her good deeds anyway.

(My cousin, Ossi, incidentally, who had to leave his parents as a child, became the mayor of Springfield, Illinois. He is now retired.)

Induction

By 1934, various German labor organizations were consolidated into the Reichsarbeitsdienst, *or RAD, the National Labor*

Service. From 26 June 1935, six months of RAD service became required for young men, prior to their compulsory military service. In the RAD, the men learned the rudiments of soldiering, while assisting in collecting the harvest, in building projects, and in agricultural land improvements. During wartime, RAD battalions also served as rear-area security troops, guarding installations, and building roads and fortifications.

Novotny was fairly unusual in that he had not been a member of the Hitler Youth prior to his RAD service. Pre-military training was an important part of Hitler Youth service, with exercises such as riflery and land navigation providing a head start to a young man's military education. These exercises made RAD and then military life easier on new soldiers, and Novotny lacked this advantage

Later in the war, the period of service was reduced to six to eight weeks, and RAD recruits sometimes manned anti-aircraft artillery pieces, much as did many Hitler Youth. RAD recruits often saw combat while on security duties, with this naturally happening more on the Eastern Front. Novotny was unlucky in seeing action in the West, during the raid by British naval and land forces on St. Nazaire, France on 28 March 1942. This operation was designed to cripple the dry docks and submarine pens. The dry dock was indeed destroyed, which made the port unusable for major German surface ships, such as the battleship Tirpitz. The submarine pens were damaged, but repaired. The British attackers lost 169 men killed and perhaps 200 captured, out of an assault force of 611.

Fred Novotny remembers . . .

By now, my homeland had become incorporated into the German *Reich* as the *"Ostmark."* Hitler's army had marched into Austria in 1938 and life became grim and hard. Even apprentices, like me, had to become *"hart"* (tough), as the Germans would say. Every company was forced to participate in the program known as *Kraft durch Freude*, "Strength through Joy."

We were up at six every morning and outside, naked from the waist up, for ten minutes of *Leibesübungen*, or calisthenics, every day, summer and winter. We were sent into the country, to help with the potato harvest, and to cheer at those massive Nazi rallies. Life had become very different as the years went by. Germany occupied Czechoslovakia, then conquered Poland, Norway, the Benelux countries, Denmark, and France, and her troops were fighting in Russia. Late in 1941, I received my call to service.

At first, there was the *RAD*, the *"Reichsarbeitsdienst,"* or Labor Service. My tour with the RAD consisted of six months of grueling service as a laborer. The RAD was only a paramilitary outfit. Every young person seventeen and a half and older was required to serve. Training in the RAD was largely strict militaristic, such as performing close-order drill without weapons. Our weapon was a spade and we were really just uniformed labor battalions.

The first month of training at *RAD Lager Lang* near Graz, Austria, were very hard for us seventeen-year-olds. It was especially stunning for me. Coming out of the luxury restaurant business, where I had been surrounded by crystal chandeliers, plush carpets, and elegantly-dressed people eating fine food, and being thrown into the tough training

RAD Group. First day in camp: *Lager* Lang near Graz, Austria, 1942.

environment there was more than a shock. Even if my youth had been spent in a relatively austere environment, being away from family, familiar friends, and surroundings forced all of us to look for substitutes. Within a very few days, friendships were formed which were to last a lifetime, or more often, "'til death us did part."

Training was hard, and our living quarters very Spartan. We faced daily forced marches of up to twenty miles. With each march, more and heavier equipment was added, too. Our training schedule had us up at 0500, training all day, and to bed at 2200. Sleeping well was no problem after days like that.

One day, we were given gas masks and told that on the next day we would don them and train with them on. I had never had such a contraption on my face. What scared me most was that we were told that training would involve real gas. Having no idea how well the masks fit and functioned was frightening.

We were ordered to put the masks on and were then herded into a room. The doors and windows were sealed, and gas

French Atlantic coast with RAD comrades, 1942. Fred Novotny in the middle. The swastika armband was a part of formal RAD uniforms, and did not reflect Nazi Party membership.

was pumped into the room. We were scared, did not do the inhaling and exhaling the way we were told, and panic set in. The room was chaos. We were let out, but this experience was repeated until we did things right. After only one day, we became comfortable with the masks, and wearing them was no longer an issue.

Weapons training followed, I remember how scary it was to hold a live hand grenade in my hands for the first time. Like the gas mask, however, soon one became familiar with all this equipment and more relaxed and sure of oneself.

Training lasted four months and transformed all individuals into a cohesive team, in which members thought and acted similarly. After we found out we were to be shipped to France, expectations and excitement were high.

We thought we were soldiers now. Little did we know better, until months later when some of us were made into soldiers of the elite Division *Grossdeutschland*, or GD. There training became really *hard,* and as we found out later during combat in Russia, for a very good reason.

We were shipped to Nantes on the French Atlantic coast to build runways. Later, we worked on huge, heavily protected

Nantes, France, 1942. The RAD's meager barracks. Novotny notes that they were building runways for the "1000 Year Reich."

U-boat pens in St. Nazaire. This was used as a staging area for raids on the Allied convoys.

One morning at 0200, the alarm sounded, klaxon horns blared, and there was a great deal of hollering and shouting. We were lined up, presented with rifles and hand grenades, and given five minutes of instruction on how to use them. We were also issued steel helmets, which, since they were much too large for our small heads, made us look ridiculous.

Apparently, the situation was serious. British commandos had landed and had created havoc. We learned the entire military garrison was on maneuvers forty miles away and we kids became overnight defenders of the U-boat bunkers. We were confused and scared, but by dawn, it was over. For reasons hard to understand, this bunch of frightened kids in their RAD uniforms succeeded in capturing many highly-trained British, even inflicting some killed and wounded.

As we found out later, the British were more surprised than we were. They had assumed that with the garrison gone, they would land, blow up their targets, and leave again. But overnight we were made into soldiers, so we were told. Two of my eighteen-year-old comrades were killed—it was our first shock of battle and baptism of fire.

From this day on, life was the same every day. Up early. Calisthenics. Breakfast. Hard work. Lunch. Hard work. Military training, which was very tough. Dinner. Then, dead tired, we would collapse into bed at 2200 and wake at 0500 to start over again.

On Sundays, if we had not fouled up during the week, we had passes which allowed us to go to town to eat some French pastries, drink beer, and gawk at the *mademoiselles.* When there were no passes to town, we would write or play chess to pass the time.

It was the first time in our lives we were so far from home—about 1,500 kilometers away, in fact. Some of us formed little groups of comrades, who became like family. Some of them I have not seen for fifty years or more, and I still remember fondly the laughter and fun we shared. One of my friends was Willy Bursch. Another was Karl Poppel.

Fred Novotny, left, and Karl Poppel on RAD service in France during 1942. They wear the arm patch of the 4th Company of RAD Battalion 365, which handled young men from eastern Austria. It is surprising that Novotny did not receive assignment to one of the RAD battalions in the 350-356 range, which were raised from the greater Vienna area.

Then, in the late summer of 1942, we were shipped home. It was wonderful to be back. Mama made all the dishes she had cooked while I was growing up, even though it was difficult to get all the ingredients. Practically everything was rationed and very scarce. People were allowed two pounds of meat per person . . . per month. There was no selection. You took whatever the butcher gave you. The rest ended up on the black market. Sugar, flour, and milk were in very short supply.

Training

Panzergrenadier Division Grossdeutschland *found its origin in the* Wachttruppe *(Guard Unit) Berlin, formed during 1934. With war looming, the unit was expanded during 1939 into an oversized infantry regiment, and given the honor title* Grossdeutschland *(Greater Germany) to reflect that its members came from every*

Reichsarbeitsdienst=Entlassungsschein

Der / Die _____ Am. _____ Alfred Novotny

geboren am __1.IV.24__ _____ in _____ Wien

war vom __8.II.42__ bis __25. Sep. 1942__ Angehörige(r) des Reichsarbeitsdienstes und am Entlassungstag Angehöriger einer im Rahmen der Wehrmacht eingesetzten Einheit*).

Er / Sie wurde am __25. Sep. 1942__ nach __Wien V, Kohlgasse 47__ zur Wiedereinstellung / vorläufig**) entlassen*).

Er / Sie hat am Entlassungstage erhalten*)

a) den Wehrpaß / Reichsarbeitsdienstpaß _____

b) Taschengeld ausgezahlt bis einschl. _____

c) Wehrsold bis einschl. __9.10.44.__

in Höhe von R.M. __30.__ monatlich,

d) Verpflegungsgeld bis einschl. __9.10.44__

e) Naturalverpflegung bzw. Lebensmittel (Urlauber-) Karten bis einschl. __26.9.42__

f) leihweise: Marschanzug, bestehend aus _____

g) Entlassungsgeld im Betrage von _____ R.M.

__Saug__, __24. Sep. 1942__

Anerkannt:

__Novotny Alfred__

Reichsarbeitsdienst
Der Führer der Abt. K 4/365 (L 502)

Oberfeldmeister u. Abteilungsführer

*) Nichtzutreffendes ist zu streichen.
**) Gilt nur für die Reichsarbeitsdienst der weiblichen Jugend (siehe Anmerkung Rückseite).

Papers issued to Novotny upon his release from RAD service.

province of Germany. In the rest of the Army, divisions were organized by region, and regiments relied on their home depots for replacements from the area each unit represented. The Infantry Regiment Grossdeutschland (GD) was selected to carry on the traditions of the Hohenzollern Imperial Guard from the Kaiser era. GD was considered the most elite unit of the German Army, even before it first saw combat during the 1940 Western Campaign. In that venue, it soon earned a fine combat reputation. The regiment also saw service in the Balkans during the spring of 1941, and in the advance on Moscow later that year. The following spring, a new, second regiment was added and the support elements expanded, creating the Infantry Division GD. This unit fought in the summer 1942 advance to the Don River, before being sent north to help defend the Rzhev salient, a German protrusion into the Soviet lines that pointed toward Moscow.

The Rzhev front held, in desperately heavy fighting, but GD was bled nearly white in the process. Novotny was one of the replacements that helped fill out the unit during a hasty replenishment after GD was returned to the southern front to help contain the Soviet offensive that had surrounded Stalingrad and recaptured much of the Donbas industrial region. Into 1941, GD consisted entirely of volunteers, and ostensibly it remained all volunteer until the end of the war. In practice, most of the replacement manpower consisted of draftees, something that is never mentioned in the divisional veterans' history compiled by German Cross in Gold and Knight's Cross recipient Helmuth Spaeter.

While Novotny was surprised to not end up in a mountain infantry unit, this was not unusual for a Viennese. Recruits for the Gebirgsjäger usually came from the mountainous regions of Austria (and Germany). Viennese commonly served in the Vienna-based 44th Infantry Division, 2d Panzer Division, and 9th Panzer Division. These units saw extremely heavy combat throughout the war, and suffered heavy casualties at a rate comparable to that of GD. The 44th Infantry Division was destroyed at Stalingrad, and Novotny entered military service at a time during which he could have easily been a founding member of the new 44th Infantry Division raised in early 1943 to replace the lost unit. This second division fought in Italy from late 1943, before being transferred to Hungary during early 1945. Had Novotny been with it, and survived, he would have ended the war close to home, as actually happened. The second 44th Infantry Division was not as highly esteemed as GD, but was still an elite unit. It distinguished itself in combat, and received the honor title "Reichsgrenadier Division Hoch und Deutschmeister (HuD)" since it maintained the traditions of that regiment, first named by Empress Maria Theresia during the eighteenth century in reference to the Austrian Emperor also holding the "HuD" title as honorary head of the Teutonic Knights. The 2d Panzer Division and 9th Panzer Division were also highly regarded units.

Fred Novotny remembers . . .

Meanwhile, back home, as the black market flourished, people became poorer and poorer, exchanging everything from art and jewelry to clothes and coins for scraps of food. At the same time, the war in Russia took its relentless toll on the German Army. Thousands upon thousands were losing their young lives in this terrible war against the massive Russian army. The Russians were not well equipped, but the elements, the winter, the numbing temperatures, the blizzards of monumental proportions, continued to batter the still proud German army.

Now, they were pushing the induction age for the army ever lower, even beneath the previous eighteen years of age. It was not surprising, therefore, that after just a few weeks at home, since I was eighteen and a half, it was my time to go. The notification came. I was to report to the training center of Division *Grossdeutschland*, the elite division of the German Army, in the town of Cottbus, southeast of Berlin.

I was shocked. I had fully expected to be drafted into one of the mostly Austrian units, such as the *Gebirgsjäger,* or mountain infantry. Many of my school buddies were assigned to such units, and they were the lucky ones. They saw an entirely different war and a few never even served in Russia.

This training was very hard for me. There was only one other Austrian in our company. I had problems understanding the drill sergeant's *Berliner* slang. Even the other enlisted men spoke a very different German than the language with which I was familiar. The drill sergeant didn't like Austrians, either. We were too soft, he felt, and he put a lot of pressure on the two of us.

As part of his bias against Austrians, this NCO must have wondered about my family name, too. After the Nazis came to power in 1938, I was not infrequently asked about it, as if it might be an indication of Slavic origin, and therefore, of unreliability or even inferiority. My grandfather was a Czech (The Czechs were part of the Austro-Hungarian Empire in his day), and the name I inherited from him, "Novotny," means "new man" in that language. I cannot recall how many times I was asked—always by upright and proud Germans—why I did not change my name to "Neumann." Such questions baffled me, but of course had their roots in the racial consciousness that was so heightened by during the Nazi era. If I were not a Slav, their reasoning went, then why would I not take the first opportunity to change my name to a properly Aryan one? Of course, later in the war, as the name Novotny/Nowotny was made famous by the *Luftwaffe* ace, Walter Nowotny, I wasn't asked this question any more.

However, the East Prussian *Feldwebel* who didn't like Austrians tried to make life more miserable than it was already. My Vienna comrade Willi Bursch (whom I met in the RAD) and I ended up spending most weekends on our hands and knees, cleaning the latrine, especially the floor there, with toothbrushes. We did this while other, more "Germanic" recruits enjoyed their passes to go into town. When we questioned the *Feldwebel* about this, his typical

Fred Novotny's
best friend during
his RAD service,
his fellow Viennese,
Willi Bürsch.

answer was, "You will go to town too, but not until we have made men of you." At this point we hated being in GD, wishing we had been assigned to an Austrian unit, such as the *Gebirgsjäger*.

Between the sheer difficulty of the training and the grief from the sergeant, I remember times I was actually crying and I wanted to go AWOL. After the first sixty days, however, I decided to show them that Austrians could take it.

There on the training ground was a man-made hill of dirt and clay. We were chased up and down this hill in full gear with machine guns and other heavy pieces of equipment. One day, after a brutal thirty minutes on the hill, my anger grew and I began to cry on the way up, certain I could not be seen by the drill sergeant. On the way down I began to grin, simply to aggravate the sergeant.

That was the day that Karl, one of the recruits, decided he could no longer take it. He shot himself in the mouth. From then on, the hill was off limits for our group.

In the second month of training, an Austrian in another company could not take the hard training and the abuse any longer, so he did the same thing. After days of commotion and blame shifting, things settled down. We became more accepted, even integrated, and slowly became regular members of what would become the division of which we would be proud.

It was just as well, too. Even without the special harassment by our *Feldwebel*, training in the GD in Cottbus tested the limits of one's endurance daily. Forced marches carrying heavy loads, long training hours, and very little sleep all induced stress. The well-prepared food helped, but there never seemed to be enough.

There were other, less comprehensible events, too. I no longer remember exactly where we started this, but for example, at some point during our training, we started a strange new routine. Stairways and doors would be closed, and we were allowed access to our barracks only via ropes hanging from second floor windows. We were also forced to climb hills all day. Rumor had it that we were trained to assault the British fortress at Gibraltar. The training lasted about three weeks, and it was exceptionally hard and exhausting. Suddenly, it stopped as suddenly as it had begun. Nothing ever came of it; we certainly never fought the British!

We never had anything resembling tactical training at all, apart from some classes on how to move while under fire. There were no squad or platoon, much less company, maneuvers or training opportunities. We route marched together, certainly, but we only learned how to move and shoot as part of a unit after we were assigned to our new units at the front.

While tactical training was not done, we did perform a great deal of close-order drill. The original units of the GD had had many ceremonial duties, so maybe this reflected in our training still, even when most of GD had become a combat outfit. The rigors of such drill did little for our battlefield abilities, but it did accomplish two things. First, long hours on the parade ground or in the barrack square are grueling physical work, so it contributed to our physical conditioning, as well as our discipline. Second, it welded us together as a team. Extended, unified movement together greatly enhanced camaraderie and teamwork. Unfortunately, we were all parceled out to different units when we arrived at the front. Nevertheless, the hard-stomping *Paradeschritt* ("Parade step," often called the "goose step" by Americans) was something we used later, even in Russia.

If we did not learn to fire our weapons in a tactical environment, there was still extensive training with all of the weapons we might eventually use as infantrymen. These included the Walther P-38 pistol, the Mauser 98 carbine, and the MG-34 and the new MG-42 (earlier and later models of machine gun). There was also individual close assault training with the MP-40 machine pistol and stick grenades. For some reason, I was much more accurate with the MG-42 than with my *Karabiner* (the standard Mauser Kar-98 bolt action rifle). I eventually became, as I was told by my instructors, a very good MG *Schütze*. I received thorough and prolonged training on the MG-42, which I had the "privilege" of carrying on my shoulders during a great deal of the time in combat to come. Later, on the front, I came to recognize how important this training was. It kept me alive.

As hard and exhausting as it was, all of this training amounted to a rite of passage that had great consequences in the months and years to come. Although we could not fully comprehend it at the time, we were being molded into a single strong, cohesive entity that would react and endure as one when we were finally subjected to the challenges of combat. Even more importantly, when GD units were worn down to only a small fraction of their original size—as happened occasionally, after particularly heavy combat—the replacements from Cottbus would arrive and fit in perfectly. This was very different from the experience of other, non-"elite" Army units during the war. In the great majority of units, by 1943 and beyond, their replacements came from many sources, quite often including fragments of entirely different outfits which were disbanded and thrown together with surviving formations.

In the GD, however, right up to the end of the war, our replacements came from our "home" depot in Cottbus, so they had already been GD soldiers for some time by the day they joined us. They had drilled like us, fired on the same ranges, lived in the same barracks, even run up and down the same hills and been yelled at by the same sergeants.

This was especially important in an outfit like GD that had so many men from places other than Germany. Whether *Volksdeutsche* (ethnic Germans) from Bessarabia, the Balkans, or the Danube Basin, or *Reichsdeutsche* from Bavaria, the Rhineland, Saxony or East or West Prussia—or even Austrians like me—we put our language and other cultural differences aside as members of the GD. Once at the front, that was all that mattered.

There was another difference between us and "average" German infantry divisions. From the time at Cottbus when we were first issued our "walking out" (semi-dress) uniforms, we wore a narrow black and silver band sewed to the cuff of our right sleeves. These black "cuff titles" had the name of our division, *"Grossdeutschland,"* embroidered on them in white (or silver, for officers), in either old-fashioned *Sütterlin* script or a more modern font. Very few other German divisions were authorized such a distinctive insignia; except for the regimental numerals on some shoulderboards, it was generally impossible to distinguish the soldiers of one unit from another in the German Army. Many *Waffen-SS* units wore cuff titles bearing their units' names on their left sleeve, and we were always quick to point out the difference; although we later learned a great respect for the battlefield prowess of several *Waffen-SS* outfits, they were not part of the German Army.

This cuff title had an important effect on us. By the addition of this simple, inexpensive device, we were not only linked more closely to each other, but were different from practically every other infantry unit in the German Army. Not just different, but, we were sure, better. We wore this insignia on our combat uniforms, too, and were glad to let anyone around us know that we were from the *Grossdeutschland!*

I recall the swearing in ceremony at GD. We pronounced an oath to Hitler, not to Germany, which seems very odd when looking back at it today. It went something like this:

> I swear by God this holy oath,
> That I am ready to serve the leader of all the German *Reich,*

The *Sütterlin* text version of the *Grossdeutschland* cuff title. (From the collection of Lieutenant Commander Ron Wolin, US Navy, Retired)

And Highest Commander of the German armed forces,
Adolf Hitler,
With unquestionable loyalty and as a brave soldier,
and am ready to lay down my life to keep this oath.

The Enemy

As long as we were in training, naturally, we were extremely
curious about the enemy we would face. Except for the
rumors about Gibraltar, there was no doubt about who we
were going to fight—the Russians. All we heard about the
Russian soldiers was that they were not educated enough to
understand their predicament, and that they were all
"*Untermenschen,*" or sub-humans. They would fight fiercely,
we were warned, because behind every line of attacking
Russians would be commissars, mercilessly shooting down
anybody trying to turn around.

Our propaganda would have had us believe the only way
for us to fight the Russians was to the death. We were told
over and over they would not take prisoners, but rather that
they would torture and subsequently shoot us if we tried to
surrender.

Our weaponry and equipment was superior, so we were
told, as was our training. As we later learned in battle, our
weapons were more precise and sophisticated, but would
not stand up to sand, mud, and the Russian winter as well as
many of the enemy's weapons. We all later scoured the bat-
tlefields for Russian-made submachine guns.

We were always hungry, but later we found out the
Russian soldier had far less to eat than we did. In combat,
one thing was confirmed: very often, only the first or second
wave of attacking Russians had weapons. The following
waves had to take them from their dead comrades.

The Russians had one particularly good propaganda
weapon, namely leaflets delivered by aircraft which told us

over and over that eventually all Germans would die on Russian soil. If this was read often enough, pretty soon one could start believing some of it. Especially from 1944 on, we grew more reluctant and less cocksure of our invincibility.

Propaganda delivered by loudspeaker was also very effective. We were told over and over that most of us would not come home. As it turned out, this was not all merely propaganda.

There was, of course, another enemy we were warned about. This enemy was one that had largely been subdued within or expelled from our homeland, we knew, but was still immensely active abroad, or so we were told. I had never been subjected to propaganda about the Jews. I was in the RAD, and since I had never been in the Hitler Youth, I have no idea what, if anything, the members of that group had to listen to. In GD, however, we were subjected to official rantings about the supposedly insidious, endless influence of the Jews in practically every aspect of the enemy's endeavors. I remember, in particular, being forced to watch a film entitled *"Der ewige Jude"* ("The Eternal Jew"), which was a filthy thing indeed. It pretended to be a documentary about the Jews in Poland, and allegedly documented Jewish culture and religion at its "secret" worst. Jews were portrayed as rats, which were overrunning the world; the ritual, kosher slaughter of a cow was not only portrayed in all its bloody horror, but was clearly portrayed as what the Jews had in mind for the rest of us.

Well, I knew for sure that Uncle Otto was no rat, and I was not sure if animals slaughtered on farms owned by good Catholics in Austria were much worse off than the one shown in the movie. It was disgusting, all right, but with the same indifference to Nazi propaganda with which we regarded the endless barrage of Communist propaganda to which we were subjected as prisoners after the war, most of us ignored this film, too. At least we were not drilling, or road marching, or climbing in and out of our barracks by rope!

After the war, we would come to recognize the monstrous crimes perpetrated by the same people who made the movie,

and maybe by many who believed it. However, our treatment as prisoners by the Soviets was not exactly gentle,
either, and it was to be years before the full truth could be
grasped. It had absolutely no effect on most of us at the time.

On to the Front

*The mass of the German Army consisted of infantry, supported by
horse-drawn artillery and wagons. As the war continued, the
armored units, being the most mobile, were shuffled around to the
crisis points, and as such, were often nicknamed* Die Feuerwehr,
*the "fire department," since they had to constantly rush to the
hotspots. For GD and for the* Waffen-SS *Panzer Divisions, this
happened even more than for other mobile formations, and GD
acknowledged the fact by using* "Die Feuerwehr" *as the title of its
division newspaper.*

Fred Novotny remembers . . .

Then came the day we awaited and feared. We were off to the
front. First, we were issued new uniforms, rifles, and gas
masks. We marched proudly through town, showing everyone what tough and hardened soldiers we had become. At
the station, we were loaded into specially-equipped cattle
cars, which were to be our homes for the next three weeks.

Food was ample. So was time. We kept ourselves groomed
and cleaned our weapons daily. We played lots of blackjack
as the train rolled eastward—a journey that was to be
reprised in a few short years, but under very different circumstances. None of us spoke of our first encounter with real
war.

We were told about our future comrades, and found it to
be true, that no other non-*Waffen-SS* unit was maintained as
well as GD. At the same time, however, no other non-*SS* unit
had so much expected of it.

Among the items provided for us were:

Choka-Cola (chocolate fortified with caffeine to keep us awake).

Butterdose (butter container made of "bakelite" ceramic, mostly filled with *"Kunsthonig"* artificial honey, not butter).

Konservenschlüssel (can opener).

Salicilspiritus, a solution for cleaning wounds.

Desitin Salbe, a salve for dressing wounds.

Traubenzucker Tabletten (grape sugar tablets for energy).

There was no doubt about it: we were very well equipped and supplied. I found the supply system within the GD always to be trustworthy, and this went a long way toward convincing us of our leaders' concern for our well-being. It was an important part of the trust and confidence we placed in them, and contributed to the bond of comradeship between leaders and led. When they ordered us to take on difficult missions, there were rarely, if ever, any sentiments other than a willingness to obey and prevail.

Combat

As eminent historian and Sovietologist David Glantz has written, after the Germans' failure to seize Moscow in the winter of 1941/42, it was obvious that the Germans could not win the war on the terms sought by Hitler. By the time Fred Novotny reached the front, this decisive point was a year in the past. The intial invasion of the Soviet Union by the Germans and their Finnish, Slovak, Hungarian, and Romanian allies had failed to put the Soviets out of the war, and massive Soviet winter counteroffensives had rocked the Germans back all along the front from the Arctic to the Black Sea.

After a German summer and autumn offensive that concentrated Axis forces in the south, in Ukraine, the Soviet Army was driven back to the Don River and, in places, to the Volga. Most threateningly, German and German-allied forces penetrated the Caucasus Mountains and advanced toward the critical oilfields in that region. With German military progress all the way to the

Egyptian frontier in north Africa, the prospect of a link up between Axis forces driving from the north and those coming from the east seemed possible for a few months in 1942.

The winter of 1942/43 ended all of that, however, as a second series of massive Soviet counteroffensives drove the Germans back into Ukraine and the Kuban Peninsula. Most importantly, Soviet operations in the late autumn and early winter of 1942 succeeded in isolating the German Sixth Army in and around Stalingrad. In the dead of a ferocious winter, this entire field army was destroyed or captured, and the other Axis forces to the north, in the Don bend and elsewhere, were shattered as well. The Italian Eighth Army, for example, was essentially destroyed, and the Hungarians and Romanians were reduced to remnants of their original strength.

As Glantz has pointed out, after Stalingrad, it became clear that the Germans would not win the war at all; the most Hitler could hope for would be some sort of military stalemate or negotiated peace. This was a war between the two great totalitarian powers of Europe, however, and the Germans were not about to give up.

Even as the mauled remains of the German Sixth Army were laying down their arms at Stalingrad, the mission of the GD was to defend in the vicinity of Kharkov. The battles, which were ultimately quite successful for the Germans, raged in that area in late January and early February 1943. The division then rested and received replacements and additional units in vicinity of Poltava, southwest of Kharkov, between 24 February and 4 March. This was the situation when Fred Novotny arrived with his comrades from Cottbus and was assigned to the 2d Company of Panzerfüsilier Regiment Grossdeutschland *(formerly the Infantry Regiment* Grossdeutschland 2, *and still often known informally by that name). As part of XLVIII Panzer Corps, GD went on the offensive 7 March 1943. The* Panzerfüsilier Regiment, *as part of* Kampf-gruppe *(Combat Group) Beuermann captured the important town of Rovni in the heaviest fighting seen by the division that day.*

Fred Novotny remembers . . .

Onward we rolled. Names of cities and regions we'd never heard of passed outside the train. Finally, we arrived at our destination. The town where we first were to meet the enemy was Poltava in Ukraine.

There were no speeches when we came to the Poltava area, straight from our training garrison in Cottbus, Germany. We were all split up, and mostly three or four new soldiers were assigned to groups of older, experienced soldiers. As was the norm in the German Army, the *Landsers* (common soldiers) with battle experience were called *Alte Hasen* (meaning "Old Hares"). I was lucky to be assigned to the group of old hare Poldi Poschusta. Later, I would realize just how lucky I was to be led by this decent, committed, and gallant young Austrian.

Even at the time, the first days at the front seemed to happen in a haze. There were so many new things: places, faces, language, fear, uncertainty, terrible battles, feeling lucky to be alive.

I think it took a few months to sink in, "You are a GD soldier now, you are with a winner." We had lots of pride and confidence up to the battle of Kursk.

We debarked at Poltava and after a night's march with full gear, we were able to rest in a heavily-wooded area. We were very restless and uncertain of how our first encounter with the enemy would go. We told one another what kind of wounds we would not like should we be hit. I was most afraid of a *Kopfschuss* (a head wound) or a *Bauchschuss* (a stomach wound). For some reason, losing a limb seemed not to be the worst, probably because we still had all of ours.

Finally, we were informed the attack would commence at 1700 hours. At 1600, all hell broke loose. Our artillery erupted, *Stuka* dive bombers screamed down, there was *flak* (antiaircraft fire) and other sorts of weaponry, all directed against the Russian lines. My thoughts flew homeward, to school and old friends, and fear grew in me about what would happen when we attacked. The minutes ticked away. The noise was fearsome, something I had never encountered before. Tanks were arriving in our attack position, adding to the smoke, the noise, and the confusion.

Then it was 1700 and we got up from our foxholes and started running toward the Russian lines, screaming *"Hurra"* as loudly as we could. The moment this happened, all fears

Fred Novotny, left front, with his fellow Fusiliers, during the late summer or autumn 1943, between the Kursk and Kiev fighting.

and thoughts of being wounded disappeared. We were all on our feet, screaming and running as one, green replacements beside old hares.

Finally, the Russians started shooting. There were machine guns, rifles, mortars, and artillery to the left and right, the screams of wounded, and the suddenly still bodies of men with whom we had spoken just moments before. We hit the first positions of the Russians and I jumped into a fox-hole to escape the artillery barrage. I could not understand that I was in there alive with so many of my comrades already dead.

The fighting was fierce. A small unit which was equipped with flamethrowers was attached to us. On our flanks and ahead of us, they burned everything in sight. The stench of burning flesh, cloth, and wood became unbearable. With the

Fred Novotny sits front left in the company of his comrades, March 1943. Standing at center is his close friend, Leopold "Poldi" Poschusta, who earned the Knight's Cross on 6 October 1943. He was killed in action on his birthday a month later, on 6 November.

screaming of the burning Russian soldiers, the whole scene was like something out of a horror movie.

I was able to move a little and the ground moved. It was not the ground or any soil, but the face of a young Russian soldier, obviously dead, lying in the foxhole with me. I will never forget his face, which seemed to be looking directly at me. It was my first hour in combat, but many more were to follow in the next horrible years.

That was my introduction to combat, sitting for hours on this dead young soldier in the foxhole into which I had jumped. I actually dozed for short periods of time on top of this young Russian, who could have been me. I have never forgotten this first impression of combat. Truly, as an American general said in 1880, "I've seen thousands of men lying on the ground, their dead faces looking up at the skies. I tell you, war is hell!"

Ordnance and Munitions

During March 1943, GD continued to advance to the northwest of Kharkov, and often had to defend against vigorous Soviet counter-attacks by units that had been cut off or bypassed by the successful German offensive. By 23 March, with Belgorod taken, GD was withdrawn to rest and prepare for the upcoming Kursk offensive.

Fred Novotny remembers . . .

The time went by. There was the hardship of living outside, exposed to the elements twenty-four hours a day, in and out of battles, losing so many good friends. It was not long before we were, at age nineteen, seasoned old soldiers, old hares ourselves.

We became familiar with how German equipment and weapons worked in the field. I always saw them as superior to the Russian equivalents. They were generally more accurate, more sophisticated. I am talking about pistols, automatic weapons, machine guns. However, this sophistication backfired often in the Russian environment of snow, ice, mud, sand. A few grains of sand in the wrong place could put a machine pistol out of commission. In the last year of the war, I switched to a Russian submachine gun, which was much more crude and the product of less exact workmanship, but was always fully functional, even under the worst conditions.

Getting ammunition for Russian weapons we used was not difficult. There was always so much left behind on the battlefield, more than we could ever use! However, it became more difficult when we were chased by the Russians, toward the end of the war. Even then, we were able to resupply because of the many counterattacks on our part, no matter how short lived. This was a practice never abandoned, even in the very last stages of the war.

I still remember the heavy boxes of ammunition for my MG-42* which, fortunately, held up quite well in Russia. Each metal box had about six belts of fifty rounds each. Very often we had three boxes with us; I carried the MG and one box, while my assistant gunner carried two boxes or more. On the longer marches, this was an extremely heavy burden, but one that was very necessary when we were attacked, which happened often in late 1943 and 1944.

I also recall how superstitious we were when it came to lighting a cigarette. No one ever took a light if two others took it before. The superstition dated back to the Great War; our fathers believed that the man who took the third light would be killed. Supposedly, it took the enemy soldier that long to line up the sights of his rifle in the dark, so that the first two to take a light would be unharmed, but the third would be shot.

---

*The MG-42 was one of the most successful weapons of the twentieth century. It featured a revolutionary simple recoil system that provided a high rate of fire and reliability. The drawback was that the MG-42, by firing at up to 1,200 rounds per minute, required enormous amounts of ammuntion, which usually had to be carried on the backs of the soldiers who used the guns or were supported by them.

Not long after I arrived at the front, I was, for some reason which still escapes me, selected for *Kradmelder* (motorcycle messenger) training. It was in the Poltava area in the Ukraine, at the beginning of 1943. I weighed less than 160 pounds, and it turned out to be quite a hard chore to handle a very heavy 750 cubic centimeter BMW machine. With all the mud, sand, and snow it was really rough. On top of it, we wore a heavy rubber coat for protection, which was very long and cumbersome.

In Russia, the life of a motorcycle messenger consisted of round-the-clock sitting and waiting, playing cards, talking, and sleeping, while awaiting the call to duty. At critical times, we always remaining totally dressed, including heavy coat and gear. We served as the liaisons between the company command post and the battalion headquarters. We always felt relatively safe at the company CP while we were waiting, but when things got hot, and the shooting and shelling began, ours was a dangerous mission. Most of the time that we were travelling back and forth between the two head-quarters we were under mortar or small arms fire, dodging the bullets and shells. Night courier duty was very bad news for us. It was impossible to use headlights, so we went in the pitch dark through snow, ice, mud, and sand. It was pretty nerve wracking, since my tour of messenger duty experience was during the worst months of winter. Road conditions were atrocious, or rather, I should ask, "what roads?" We often created them through our driving. Fortunately, this stint lasted only three months; heavy casualties forced us to be reassigned to line units and regular combat infantry duties. I returned to my MG-42.

———————————

There came a curious interlude here which I still ponder. It happened in a small village near Kharkov, where we stumbled out of the cold rain into a two-room *"dacha,"* which the inhabitants had abandoned. It was a dark hovel with a smooth mud floor, and a Russian-style oven surrounded by a sleeping area. The second room was dark with a heavy velvet drape over a small window, with a table in the middle, two chairs, a dresser, and on top, an old-fashioned RCA gramophone. We found a single 78 rpm disc there, and to my surprise, it was a recording of "Stormy Weather." This was the music I had grown up with since I was fifteen years old! My father liked Strauss and Lehar, but I liked Louis Armstrong and Harry James. So here we were in this dark little cabin in the depths of Russia listening to "Stormy Weather" and crying with the memories it evoked.

The question still puzzles me today. Here in this poor homestead in the middle of the Ukraine was an American gramophone, and a single record. What life story might exist behind this simple occurrence?

This and other events have also caused me, in the years after the war, to muse about the term "enemy." It was a word indoctrinated into the minds of young soldiers on all sides, in Germany, Russia, America, and elsewhere. With this word, we could kill one another without a thought. We did not

Poltava, Ukraine, 1943. Relaxing in the cold April sun in front of a *"dacha"* shortly before attacking enemy lines. Fred Novotny sits at left front. Notice the *Grossdeutschland* cuff-title on the arm of the man above him.

know each other, we rarely saw each other at close range until a battle was over, but we were all trained to fight and to kill one another, and millions of us "enemy haters" got killed.

Interestingly, veterans of the Western Front, Italy, and North Africa have told me, since the war, that they often referred to their adversaries as *die Gegner*, or "the opponents." This is the same term used in sporting situations, and if this is true, it certainly reflects a major difference between how they viewed the men across the lines from them. On the Eastern Front, we called them *der Feind*, "the enemy," and it was no sporting matter, I can tell you.

Kursk and Beyond

When the spring 1943 thaw set in, the Soviets still held a salient extending into the German lines north of Belgorod. This was similar to the German-held Rzhev salient of the previous year, and the German plan for the summer of 1943 was to destroy this bulge in their lines before pursuing further aims. GD was part of a powerful force ordered to attack from the south, while a less powerful force attacked from the north. Both sides knew where the German attacks were coming, and the Soviets built extremely strong defenses to counter them.

GD was reinforced by the first operational unit of Panther tanks, Panzer Regiment 39 under Knight's Cross holder Meinrad von Lauchert. This was attached to the Panzer Regiment GD, which had distinguished itself in the Kharkov campaign under the command of the "Panzer Graf," Hyazinth Graf (Count) Strachwitz von Gross-Zauche und Camminetz. Count von Strachwitz had earned the Oakleaves to his Knight's Cross on 18 March 1943, and was highly regarded within GD. Lauchert was also a capable commander, and he and von Strachwitz did not get along well during their forced cooperation, with each blaming the other for the failures of the GD armored forces during the Kursk fighting.

Despite valiant efforts, GD made only minimal advances during Operation ZITADELLE ("CITADEL"), and at the cost of heavy casualties. The commander of the Panzerfüsilier Regiment, *Erich Kassnitz, was mortally wounded on 5 July 1943, and died on 29 July. He had been awarded the Knight's Cross two weeks earlier for his regiment's initial success in capturing the heights around Gerzovka, on GD's left flank.*

As David Glantz has noted, after Kursk, it was obvious that Germany would, in fact, lose to the Soviets; it was only a matter of time.

Fred Novotny remembers . . .

Then came the summer of 1943 and we were destined to be a part of one of the great battles of the war. It was the battle of Kursk, where the German *OKW* (*Oberkommando der Wehrmacht,* or high command), planned a massive offensive at the beginning of July. This was Operation *ZITADELLE.*

I remember is how much talk there was among us that we had "nothing to fear," because we had Graf von Strachwitz and his new, invincible Panther tanks with us. After the war, I heard that there had been some recriminations between the famous and respected Strachwitz and the attached Panther battalion commander, Meinrad von Lauchert. Of course, at no time during the actual fighting at Kursk did we at the lower levels ever know of problems between them.

We were, however, all told of the capabilities of this great new tank, that it was better than the T-34 and KV series tanks very much feared by us.

The knowledge among the *Panzerfüsilier Regiment* that our neighbor was GD 1 (the Grenadier Regiment) and Strachwitz's tanks kept us very confident, until a few days into the actual fighting. We were shocked to experience the real strength of the Russian troops and their armor.

The first hours of the Kursk offensive still cause flashbacks fifty-odd years later. Sometimes I think I can still hear the incredibly loud noise of the German weapons, including flak, artillery, mortars, *Stukas,* and *Nebelwerfers* (multiple rocket launchers); I cannot forget the endless, terrible downpour of rain, rain, and more rain. We were totally drenched, heavily laden down with equipment, knee deep in mud all around us, and filled with the great uncertainty of what lay ahead.

I remember clearly, after our encounters with the Russians around Kharkov, and the subsequent battles around the Donets, the feeling of invincibility had only been reinforced in all of us. Regardless of the beating the Paulus Army took in Stalingrad, of which we were told very little, our spirits were high because of our own success against the Russians. So high were our spirits that we did a lot of singing while marching. One of the most common songs, *Graue Kolonnen* ("Grey Columns"), while melancholy, was also quite inspiring, as it not only seemed written for our own situation, but harkened to our fathers' similar experiences in the Great War.

"GRAUE KOLONNEN"	"GRAY COLUMNS"
Graue Kolonnen	Gray columns
Zieh'n in der Sonne	March in the sun,

Oberst Hyazinth *Graf* (Count) Strachwitz von Gross-Zauche und Camminetz, who commanded the panzer regiment of GD during Operation *ZITADELLE*. This photo depicts him later in the war, wearing the Knight's Cross with Oakleaves and Swords. (National Archives)

Oberstleutnant Meinrad von Lauchert, who commanded the battalion of Panthers attached to the GD during Operation *ZITADELLE*. (National Archives))

Müde durch Heide und Sand	Tiredly, through heath and sand;
Neben der Straße	Beside the road
Blühen in Grase	Bloom in the grass
Blumen am Wegesrand	Flowers along the roadside.
Blumen am Wege, wie blüht ihr so schön!	Flowers along the way, how beautifully you bloom!
Aber wir dürfen ja stille nicht steh'n	But we cannot stand still
Wenn wir marschieren in Feindesland!	When we march on enemy soil!
Wenn wir marschieren in Feindesland!	When we march on enemy soil!
Ruhlos in Flandern	Restless in Flanders
Müssen wir wandern	We must wander
Weit von der Heimat entfernt	Far away from the homeland;

Graue Soldaten	Gray soldiers
Im Schrei der Granaten	Have forgotten laughter
Haben das Lachen verlernt	In the shriek of shells;
Ob auch zu Hause ein Mädel wohl weint	Even if a girl may cry at home,
Draußen im Felde schon wartet der Feind	Out in the field, the enemy already waits,
Wenn wir marschieren in Feindesland!	When we march on enemy soil!
Wenn wir marschieren in Feindesland!	When we march on enemy soil!
Vorwärts die Blicke	Look only forward,
Niemals zurücke	Not ever back
Geht unser Marsch an die Front	So goes our march to the front;
Über den Gräben	Above the trenches
Über dem Leben	Above the life,
Einsam ein Kamerad thront	a lonely comrade ascends,
Kamerad Tod, du winkst uns schon zu	Comrade Death, you wave to us already
Aber wir wollen den Sieg und nicht Ruh'	But we want Victory and not quiet,
Wenn wir marschieren in Feindesland!	When we march on enemy soil!
Wenn wir marschieren in Feindesland!	When we march on enemy soil!

We were totally convinced as soldiers that Kursk would turn the war around again, in favor of Germany. We, the Fusiliers and Grenadiers, would do it! Perhaps this feeling was not shared at headquarters, however, for they knew much more about the Russian forces' situation than we did.

For us, the major battle began at 1400 hours on 4 July. It quickly turned into an inferno as tanks, troops, airplanes, and artillery were flung into the action. The sky opened and it poured rain, turning the ground into a sea of mud. It was difficult to move on foot, and almost impossible to make way in a motorized vehicle. After three days of heavy fighting, we attacked the main Russian strongholds with all we had. Hand-to-hand combat ensued as the Russians defended their territory with a determined ferocity.

I was near total exhaustion, running downhill and carrying my weapon. I heard bullets all around me, but with the adrenaline rush, there was no sense of fear or time to think. As I was throwing myself to the ground headfirst, bullets made sounds like little crickets all around me. I felt a blow to my head. I felt no pain, but as I reached up to my head, I cut my my hand on jagged metal. A bullet had hit my steel helmet and traveled all around my head, tearing off the helmet's rim, but not causing a scratch on my scalp.

Frantically, I clung to the ground; with my hands, I dug a hole just big enough for my head to fit in and covered up with what was left of my helmet. Some bullets still pelted the ground where I lay, so I dug in deeper. Bullets tore into my pack, then I felt something hit my lower left leg. There was no pain for the moment, but seconds later, I felt a searing, burning sensation. Without lifting my head, I ran my left hand down my left leg, and felt inside my boot. When I withdrew it, it was completely covered in blood. Now the pain grew stronger. I began to panic, not knowing quite what had happened, and I called out for a *Sani* (*Sanitäter*, or medic).

The next thing I knew, I was in a field hospital. They told me that I had been hit by nine bullets, only one of which actually wounded me. The rest were stuck in my equipment, including the one in my helmet. It was more than a lucky break. Someone was looking out after me.

So, I was away from the front for a while. After ten days, I was transported to a hospital in Freudenthal, which was then occupied Czechoslovakia. As it turned out, my father was on leave from his Army assignment in France. He was one of those unlucky ones to be born in 1900, so even though he had already served in World War I, he was recalled to the colors this time around, too. Fortunately, he was detailed as a supply truck driver in France. One day, he simply appeared at the end of my bed in the hospital. As he sat on my bed and we exchanged small talk, he yanked the covers back. A relieved smile spread across his face and he squeezed me again and again. He was so convinced that I had lost one, or both legs, that he could not bring himself to ask me. He said my letter to home had made little of my wound, so they expected the worst.

This wounded tag was affixed to Novotny on 7 July 1943 by the first medic who found him for the leg injury he received.

Befitzeugnis

Dem

Füs. Alfred Novotny

[Name, Dienstgrad]

2.Kp. Rgt. 2, Div. Großdeutschland

[Truppenteil, Dienststelle]

ift auf Grund

feiner am ...... *7. 7. 1943* ...... erlittenen

*ein*malige Verwundung — Befchädigung

das

Verwundetenabzeichen

in ...... *Schwarz* ......

verliehen worden.

Freudenthal, den ...... *24. 8.* 19 *43.*

....

[Unterfchrift]

Oberftabsarzt u. Chefarzt

[Dienftgrad und Dienftftelle]

Fred Novotny's certificate for the Wound Badge in Black, presented on 28 August 1943, for his first wound, suffered weeks earlier
at Kursk on 7 July.

Then I was sent back home for a twelve-day leave. I had
not seen my mother or sister for over a year and a half. There
was such joy. Mama was so happy, always asking me what I
wanted to eat, even though they had almost nothing. As a
wounded soldier, I had a little better ration card than

civilians, one that even authorized some more meat. So Mama went shopping and we had a great feast.

My parents no longer lived in our old, familiar apartment. It had been bombed and they moved into a smaller place. There simply was no other choice.

After telling them what I had been doing over the past eighteen months, I took a day to look up the parents of my five best friends to see how they were faring. As it turned out, by a rare coincidence, we were all home on leave at the same time. We could not believe it. Rudy was with the *Gebirgsjäger* and had lost his left hand. Hans had lost his right arm. Poldi (short for Leopold) lost both legs below the knee, and Fritz was home because his brother had been killed. Pepi, we heard, was missing in action. We had a great couple of days together telling each other about our experiences, our horrors, but were still happy to be alive.

It was almost time to leave and things became very quiet at home. The mood was somber. We did not know when we would see each other again, if ever. Papa had to leave for

My first-grade school friends at their only meeting, Vienna, 1943, during the height of the war.

France. Luckily, he was sent home six months later, but we were not to see each other for many years.

The Withdrawal from Ukraine to Romania

*Novotny was fortunate to miss the fighting that immediately fol-
lowed Operation ZITADELLE. The German units were not able to
replace their losses from the offensive, and were further worn down
in successive defensive stands and counterattacks against the
resurgent Red Army forces that drove for the Dnepr River. From
this point on, the Soviet numerical superiority in manpower and
weaponry never diminished. Motorized units such as GD suffered,
but far less than the many infantry divisions, which were often cut
off by Soviet advances, and had to retreat as best they could on foot.*

*By autumn 1943, the German armies had been forced out of
much of Ukraine, and had abandoned Kiev. The front briefly stabi-
lized near Zhitomir, west of Kiev, as German armored reserves
launched a partially successful counteroffensive in November.*

*GD fought southeast of Kiev at this time. It retreated first to the
Kremenchug bridgehead, along the Dnepr upriver from Dnepro-
petrovsk, before retreating south to the vicinity of Krivoi Rog. From
there, the division moved west to the Kirovograd sector in early
1944. It was at this time, on 27 January 1944 that* Generalleutnant *Hasso von Manteuffel replaced Oakleaves recipient
Walter Hoernlein as the GD's commanding general. GD possessed
only a fraction of its pre-*ZITADELLE *strength at this time, and only
a few replacements, mainly recovered wounded such as Novotny,
were received. There was no chance for GD to be withdrawn for any
substantial rest and replenishment.*

*The constant withdrawals did not mean that the Soviets had an
easy time recapturing Ukraine. Their forces were consistently successful, but at a high cost in men and armored vehicles.*

*One of the German soldiers responsible for the Soviets' difficul-
ties in taking back Ukraine was Fred's superior,* Unteroffizier
Leopold Poschusta. The 2d Company of the Füslier Regiment GD,
to which Poschusta and Novotny were assigned, was operating in

the sector of the 23d Panzer Division on 6 October 1943. On his own initiative, Poschusta broke up a Soviet assembly area with a quick strike, before the enemy could form for an attack. He was thanked in an order of the day issued by the 23d Panzer Division two days later. Poschusta was killed in action a month later, on 6 November 1943.

Fred Novotny remembers . . .

Back to the front. I was with my regiment again, south of Kiev in the Ukraine, in the vicinity of Kremenchug and around the Dnepr River. Fighting went on daily, in great, confused battles in which terrain was lost, regained, lost, and taken back again. General von Manstein directed the German armies and the Russians were led by Generals Koniev, Tolbukhin, and Malinovsky, all highly decorated and capable.

There were repeated battles around the city of Krivoi Rog, with heavy losses on both sides. The winter was beginning to close in.

It was during this period, when defeat began to loom over us for the first time, that Leopold Poschusta demonstrated his great strength of character and courage. When I first met him, before Kursk, he was a *Gefreiter*, and we talked a lot about Austria, our friends, our parents, and the good food. This calm, reliable, trustworthy man became my good friend. We liked to play an old, simple Austrian card game, and we played it every free minute because it took our minds off of the grim day-to-day war. The game was called *Schapsen* and is still played today. Poldi liked to win, but did not lose his temper if he lost. He merely said, "I will win the next one," and then proceeded to do so.

He was always helpful with deeds and advice, having been at the front for some time already. Our whole group looked up to him, because of his cool handling of many tight situations and for keeping our spirits high by his words and actions.

Elements of the 2d Company of *Panzerfüsilier Regiment Grossdeutschland* on the march during 1943. At right, holding his cap, is "Poldi" Poschusta.

After one such action near Krivoi Rog, around an old airstrip, where his initiative helped to keep a strong Russian attack at bay, he was promoted to *Unteroffizier* and subsequently was assigned as a *Zugführer* (platoon leader). Rumors flew that Poldi might be awarded the *Ritterkreuz.* Later, they proved to be true. How proud we were to be part of his group. According to what we heard, he was to be pulled out of combat for awhile and be presented to new GD recruits in Cottbus and Guben to boost morale!

One day during only desultory fighting, the word spread—"Poldi's been killed." It was true; he was actually killed on his birthday. We were in shock, our hero and pillar of strength was gone! His award of the *Ritterkreuz* was posthumous.

I always remember this gentle, heroic Austrian friend I had for a few months in my life.

Years later, back in Austria after returning from prison camp, whenever I heard over the radio the song *"Ich hatt' einen Kameraden,"* I thought only of Poldi Poschusta. What an impression he had made on me, this teenaged warrior. My eyes always became wet when I heard this haunting melody and sad words.

"ICH HATT' EINEN KAMERADEN"	"I HAD A COMRADE"
Ich hatt' einen Kameraden,	I had a comrade,
Einen bessern findst du nit.	You won't find a better one.
Die Trommel schlug zum Streite,	The drum called us to fight,
Er ging an meiner Seite	He went by my side,
Im gleichen Schritt und Tritt,	In the same pace and step.
Im gleichen Schritt und Tritt.	In the same pace and step.
Eine Kugel kam geflogen:	A bullet flew towards us,
Gilt's mir oder gilt es dir?	Is it for me or for you?
Ihn hat es weggerissen,	It tore his life away,
Er liegt mir vor den Füßen	He lies now at my feet,
Als wär's ein Stück von mir.	As though a part of me
Als wär's ein Stück von mir.	As though a part of me
Will mir die Hand noch reichen,	His hand reached up to hold mine.
Derweil ich eben lad'.	Even as I am re-loading.
"Kann dir die Hand nicht geben,	"I can't give you my hand,
Bleib du im ew'gen Leben	You remain in eternal life,
Mein guter Kamerad!	My good comrade!
Mein guter Kamerad!"	My good comrade!"

The weather was absolutely horrible even before the onset of full winter. After days of marching in rain, sleet, mud and snow, our uniforms became rags. As the leather of our boots remained soaked for weeks at a time, the stitching decayed and the soles came loose. At one point, we had not seen the inside of a house or bunker for a full month. We all tried to protect ourselves as well as we could.

We covered our heads with scarves, or what was left of them, and we wrapped our feet in every available piece of rag. Our uniforms were replaced only on the rare occasions we were pulled out of the front. We stayed drenched and cold for too long, and became thoroughly numb. The immersion foot and, in some places, frostbite that occurred on my feet and legs is still a great bother to me, and remains the cause of many visits to the doctor. In a way, though, I am lucky; at least I still have my feet, with all toes intact. Many of my comrades cannot say the same.

There is a name from this period that is always on my mind, mainly because of our ever-so-short acquaintance. Walter Grube was a handsome nineteen-year-old from Berlin (as I later found out), and he came to our sector of the front as a replacement from Cottbus. He was ordered by our sergeant to share a foxhole with me and I was glad. He jumped in, extended his hand and said, "I am Walter Grube." At that very moment, an artillery shell landed in our foxhole between him and the wall and he was literally blown apart. I had not even had a chance to tell him my name. I was not even scratched.

I was in shock. For six decades, I have tried to figure out why I was spared and he, who had not spent a single minute at the front, had to die. There are no answers to such things, of course; at least, not on this side of eternity. Still, I cannot help wondering.

In January, we were were pulled out and moved further west. We were entrenching, digging foxholes, and building other fortifications to make a stand against what were by now bigger and more powerful Russian units, constantly being thrown against us. The manpower ratio at that point was about five to one in favor of the Russians. In our sector, at least, there seemed to be a similarly overwhelming ratio of weapons, tanks, artillery, and airplanes. By now, we could discern that the Russians were getting a great deal of help from America. Most of the trucks we captured were Studebakers, fresh from America. When we saw American equipment on the battlefield, such as those Studebaker trucks, we were impressed with the ruggedness of it. Had we have known how much Russia got from America, we would surely have worried a lot! Actually, at our age, we had no concept of the real strength of the American war machine. Therefore, we gave no thought to it.

Then came weeks of marching, digging in, and fighting, with the Russian Army always a single night's march behind us. We would march twenty-five to thirty kilometers nightly, halt at 0400, and dig in again.

Food was becoming scarce. One day, we found a three-hundred-pound barrel of honey in a barn. We were half starved and used our hands and anything we could find to scoop out the honey. We were sticky all over, and finally we gave up. The honey froze as hard as granite. Still, it was great while we could eat it.

The conditions began to became unbearable and some of us began talking about surrender, saying that prisoner of war camps couldn't be worse. We talked about how we had lost the war and our complaints obviously were the sign of a disintegrating army. We were told that anyone staying behind who fell into Russian hands, however, would be tortured, have their fingernails torn out, their ears cut off and so forth. Not only were we frustrated, but we were scared. I was twenty, and I was convinced that I was too young to die.

The marching and digging went on and on. The weather was impossibly brutal. I became so tired that I hardly cared any more. My feet were beginning to show signs of frostbite and I was in agony. My sergeant, Karl, was marching in front of me, and I told him, "Karl, I have to sit down. I cannot go on any more." He just kept walking. Several times I repeated myself, "Karl I cannot go on any more." I was becoming angrier and angrier. Tears were running down my cheeks. I threw my rifle to the ground, yanked off my equipment and sat down, shivering and crying, crazy with anger and hate. "Karl, Karl," I kept calling. Slowly, he looked back and said, "We might make it, we might make it if we go on, but I know for sure you won't."

With all my power, I got myself up again and got going. We marched another fourteen kilometers, even though I had felt thirteen kilometers ago that I could not take another step and that I had spent myself completely. We humans are much tougher than we think.

Later, I told Karl again and again how grateful I was that he made me get up and move on. We stayed in touch for forty-five years after the war. He died in 1990.

To add to the temptation of desertion, the Russians directed several types of propaganda against us frontline soldiers. First, the loudspeakers, which often seemed to be only meters away from our lines, told us very accurately in German sentences such as, "You know, you all will rot in Russia. Have your leaders learned nothing from Napoleon's horrendous defeat? We ask you, stop fighting, come over to us! Join the brotherhood of men under Socialism." Or, alternatively, they said, "Do not continue Hitler's war. Remember, Ivan is coming! Put down your weapons now and live, you are too young to die!"

To us, these were very powerful words, ones which could not be completely ignored. We had many discussions among us, trying to convince ourselves that everything the Russians said were lies. Nevertheless, hearing what were clearly the voices of Germans had a serious impact on us. We had no idea at the time, of course, about the *Komitee Freies Deutschland* (the "Committee of Free Germany"). This was a group which included genuinely anti-Hitler officers, turncoat soldiers looking for better treatment, and a few misguided idealists—captured German soldiers all—who were dominated by a group of German Communists who had fled to the USSR after the Nazi takeover in 1933. They often participated in the propaganda broadcasts, and despite the already low temperatures, it was chilling to be addressed in perfect German by our comrades, inviting us to give up and "take it easy" as guests of the Red Army.

On the other hand, we were also unknowingly under the constant influence of our own propaganda, describing the Russians as "*Untermenschen*," incapable of ever defeating an army or division like ours. This was pretty hard stuff for eighteen- to twenty-year-olds to digest.

The Russians also used printed propaganda delivered from above, leaflets dropped by the tens of thousands. These inevitably included photos of captured Germans and the words of our own comrades, encouraging us to lay down our weapons. We were also bombarded with leaflets saying, in essence, "Because Hitler does not have enough people to match the great Soviet population, and because Hitler has no more reserves of troops, unlike the Soviets, you ought to surrender." Each leaflet had a stamp on it saying, "*Passierschein*," which was a free pass to surrender and be treated fairly. All the leaflets were specifically addressed "To the Soldiers of GD."

As tempting as many of the leaflets were, sometimes, they were stilted and silly. On one side, it said something like, "Because of your occasional success, you are a *Kriegsverlängerungsdivision* (war-prolonging division); come over to our side and become a *Kriegsverkürzungsdivision* (war-curtailing division). Our officers must have had their hands full convincing us that all was well. We were a highly-trained and motivated group of young lions, however, and in the end, we always ended up believing in our invincibility and superiority.

This kind of propaganda made us think very hard; we could not dismiss it completely. Our counterpropaganda, however, explained to us that it was just desperate moves by the Soviets. Since they could not defeat us in battle, they instead tried to beat us by spreading untrue stories. We must have believed our own propaganda more, since we kept fighting on.

I remember that well into 1944, I finally heard of one of our soldiers deserting. It happened in another company and I did not personally know the fellow who went over. It was a major scandal, and we were all horrified that a GD man would do such a thing. Despite all the pain, all the fear, and all the propaganda, when one of us actually deserted, most of us really couldn't imagine doing the same thing.

Although propoganda could sometimes be discouraging, there was another phenomenon that was downright frightening. We never liked being opposed by Russian penal units. Thousand of these soldiers were driven toward us by commissars with pistols drawn, with nothing to lose, or very little hope of survival, and so these outcasts fought ferociously. Their never ending shouts of "*Hurra! Hurra!*" I remember to this day. I had heard that the German armed forces had

similar units—they were called units "for special employ-
ment," but I never personally encountered any of them. The
Russians must have been as terrified by them as we were by
theirs.

As the war went on in late 1943 and 1944, the German
Army must have lost an enormous amount of fighting men.
This was also true with our division. Marching back, digging
in, our foxholes were spread farther and farther apart, often
instilling a great uneasiness. Realizing that the adjacent hole
might be seventy-five to one hundred meters away was not
only damaging to our morale, but was bad for our nerves,
too, because of hardly any communication with the next man
over was possible.

I remember one such night in the midst of winter, we were
dug in on a ridge only knowing that there were other comrades dug in left and right of us, but we could hardly see
each other. I was positioned behind my MG-42, my assistant
gunner next to me sleeping. We woke each other up every
one hour to take guard duty.

Heavy snow blanketed the area and everything was eeri-
ly quiet. All of a sudden, the soldiers in the hole on our left
fired a flare, illuminating the area in front of us, and immediately began shooting as fast as they could. A field of bodies
in white camouflage winter uniforms were quickly crawling
toward our lines. I kicked my buddy and started blindly firing my MG-42 without stopping for at least three minutes.

Fire broke out from all our foxholes, two tanks were moving into position behind us, soon firing down the hill. My
MG was very hot from all that non-stop firing. It was about
0400 when the Russians started attacking. By daybreak,
around 0700, we could see what was in front of us. Hundred
of dead Russians were piled on top of each other, the snow
red with blood. Some Russians had managed to come as
close as seven meters or less. Miraculously, our company had
suffered only three men wounded. Some wounded were
Russians were picked up by our troops in the morning. They
told us it was their first day in combat. Some were not even
sixteen years old.

Additionally, a long forgotten heart stopper comes to mind. It was winter and Poldi Pochusta, my good friend, had been killed, a truth very hard to swallow. This calm pillar of strength, who could keep the men relaxed with his reassuring personality, was gone. How could we survive? Someone else took over the platoon, I can't remember his name, nor can I recall the face. We were assigned to go on a patrol to bring in one or more Russian prisoners for interrogation.

With the snow knee deep, walking was a nightmare. We left most of our equipment behind, to avoid giving ourselves away with the clutter. All we took were our weapons, mainly machine pistols and hand grenades.

We were out for about one hour, our winter uniforms making us hard to see in the snow. We continued to hunt for Russians. Suddenly, the patrol leader signaled us to stand completely still, and we heard Russian voices . . . behind us. There were eight of us; we split up and hit the ground behind tree trunks covered high with snow. The blood was pounding in my ears, and I assume that everyone else's was too. We had no idea how many Russians were behind us, or how they had gotten there, in effect cutting us off from our lines.

The Russians were silent now, within shooting range, but we didn't know how many were out there. I thought to myself, "How did the hunters become the hunted?"

As they came into sight, we counted six. To our amazement, two had their hands above their head. Four Russians had gone on patrol with the same orders we had, to bring back some prisoners. As the group passed between us, we jumped up screaming, "Hands up!"

One Russian started firing, not knowing we were on both sides. He was hit by our bullets and fell, and the others surrendered. The two German soldiers from another infantry unit could not get over their luck! More surprisingly, one of the Russian prisoners said to us, "Thank you for capturing me!" We could only imagine the conditions in his own army if those were truly his feelings. We got back to our lines without sustaining friendly casualties, and accomplished our mission. We were greatly relieved to be back in our own lines, as things did not always work out as well as they had in this case.

Homelands

German propaganda often portrayed Russians and other Slavs as subhumans, and the Soviet Union as a Bolshevist menace in need of destruction. The impression the Soviet Union and its people made upon German soldiers has been recorded in many books and preserved letters. Their disgust at the often primitive conditions and at a government that would allow such squalor often seems an echo of the propaganda. In fact, few German soldiers were openly pro-Nazi, and no propaganda was needed to convince the majority that they represented a more advanced culture, one which would suffer greatly if the Soviets ever occupied Germany. German soldiers, including Novotny, came to realize how much they treasured their homeland, and they continued until the end of the war to risk their lives to protect it.

Fred Novotny remembers . . .

Heimat. This word would create a feeling of euphoria, sadness, and pride. Our *Heimat* was what we were fighting for, living for, and dying for. Speaking or hearing this word would evoke a strong feeling and longing, of wanting to be home, in familiar surroundings, with family and friends! The German word for that sensation is *"Heimweh."*

Two songs I remember would trigger *Heimweh* like nothing else. Number one was *"Hast Du Dort oben vergessen auf Mich?"* It is an appeal to God, meaning in English something like, "Have You up there forgotten me?" The lyrics of this sad song started as follows, *"Es steht ein Soldat am Volga strand, hält wache für sein Vaterland"* (Along the Volga as a soldier I stand, posting watch for the fatherland). And then the chorus, *"Hast Du Dort oben vergessen auf Mich?"*

The second song was, "*Unrasiert und fern der Heimat, fern der Heimat unrasiert*," or, "Unshaven and far, far from home, far far from home and unshaven," with the lines repeated again and again.

The reason I mention this is because I think the feelings were uniquely German. And strangely enough, we as soldiers in Russia were actually worried about winning the war, and then standing guard for all our young lives, far far away from our *Heimat*. God knows for how long, no returning home for us, to enjoy what we fought and suffered for. As it turned out, history had something else for us in mind. We lost the war, suffered more for it, and standing guard on the Volga became the least of our worries!

During our long years in the Soviet Union, naturally, we had a great deal of contact with the civilian population. We heard that when the first German troops arrived in Ukraine in 1941, they were genuinely greeted as liberators by most of the inhabitants. Of course, we had all seen the newsreels of those exciting days, but now that we knew more about our own propaganda, it was difficult to judge just how glad the inhabitants had really been. Nevertheless, by mid- to late 1943, on the surface, at least, the Ukrainian women (we called them "*Madgas*") were very helpful and friendly, always cursing the Communists. What their real feelings were, we could not really know. We quickly learned, as we slept in their homes, that they were in great need of the simplest things, such as yarn, needles, matches, buttons, and so on.

These were all things we could often provide, in turn we would get bread, eggs on occasion, and even sometimes some milk. Salt was another thing they needed and that we were able to procure from our own stores.

We often had long conversations, and they would tell us of the hardships living under Communism, and the moving fates of the families who would spend months and years in Soviet prisons, because Ukrainians were not trustworthy people in the eyes of the Russians. I remember the first words we would learn were the names for food items. "*Curitza*" for chicken, *"khleba"* for bread, *"yaikas"* for eggs, *"moloka"* for milk, and so on.

When frontline conditions allowed it, we were able to find shelter in Ukrainian homes, small huts with mud walls and small windows. It was a good news/bad news situation, sleep outside and freeze, or sleep inside and be devoured by bedbugs and lice. The standards of hygiene were astonishingly different from those of even poor German or Austrian civilians at the time.

The huts were built around the most important feature, the big sleeping/heating/cooking oven in every home. Being on a bed above the fire was very warm and cozy, but bed bugs and lice would crawl into your hair. They would have a field day in your face, sucking blood from your mouth, nose, and nostrils. As I said, it was either freeze and don't sleep or be warm and tortured. It was not a great choice!

Later, in prison, I faced similar problems. Wooden barracks with wooden ceilings and walls, crawling with bedbugs. Bedbugs would fall on you all night, and the rooms were full of mice, seeking shelter from the icy cold. Head lice became a problem if your hair grew even a little. So, the Russians shaved our heads, but this caused other problems; the lack of hair then made staying warm much more difficult, as fifty percent of body heat escapes from the head!

Soldiers of *Grossdeutschland*

Being the "fire department" meant that a unit was usually in the worst situations, but also that it was normally soon withdrawn, to rest and rebuild before being sent to another crisis. Normal, unmotorized infantry divisions rarely had this luxury. They grew resentful of all mobile units, whether Army or Waffen-SS. Elite units develop a proud sense of camaraderie, one that is best understood by similar elites. This is why the men of GD, who were in a sense the rivals of the Waffen-SS in the sphere of guarding Hitler and other highly-placed personalities, came to see the Waffen-SS armored units as their best comrades at the front. The 3d SS-Panzer

Division Totenkopf *fought alongside GD from the late summer of 1943 until the late spring of 1944, and these two divisions were full of praise for each other. It is noteworthy that in his divisonal history, Spaeter has nothing but scorn for the SS-Kavallerie Division, which was far less elite than the* Waffen-SS *armored divisions.*

Non-German Axis forces on the Eastern Front were a mixed lot. Certain formations, especially Romanian units in the Crimea, fought well. However, most non-Germans had little desire to be on the Eastern Front, and they also usually lacked modern equipment and weaponry.

Within GD, the two infantry regiments did not like one another. Each had derogatory nicknames for the other, and the animosity occasionally hampered combined operations. By 1944, most leadership positions within GD were filled by competant officers who did not originate with GD, and who could put the military good ahead of petty squabbles.

Horst Niemack commanded an infantry reconnaissance battalion during the first two years of the war, earning the Knight's Cross during the Western Campaign, and the Oakleaves the next year. He was awarded the Swords to his Knight's Cross during the Bessarabian fighting as the commander of Panzerfüsilier Regiment GD.

Hans-Dieter von Basse was Novotny's battalion commander. Their unit, the 1st Battalion of Panzerfüsilier Regiment GD, *was reformed after the spring 1944, fighting from a truck-borne unit to one mounted on armored halftracks. Von Basse earned the German Cross in Gold during the retreat from Ukraine, and received the Knight's Cross for leading his battalion in Lithuania during August 1944.*

Hasso Eccard Freiherr *von Manteuffel was an experienced cavalryman and tanker, and came from a* Junker *family. He won the Knight's Cross as a regimental commander in the 7th Panzer Division, and later won the Oakleaves as the commander of that division. While in command of GD, he was awarded the Swords for an earlier success with the 7th Panzer Division. Long-time GD commander Walter Hoernlein was the most revered by his men, but von Manteuffel, who held command for seven months during 1944, was the most respected for his leadership and abilities.*

Eugen Garski was the first commander of Regiment GD2. He had earned the Knight's Cross with Regiment GD in the Western Campaign, and was killed in action during the Rzhev fighting.

Fred Novotny remembers . . .

My war experiences are inevitably heavily influenced by the fact that I was a member of an elite unit. As part of 2d Company, *Panzerfüsilier Regiment* GD, we always felt superior to other units, and were even convinced that we were better than GD1 (the Grenadier Regiment), although this was not always true. There were many battles and skirmishes where GD1 had to come to GD2's help and bail us out. As much as we liked being in GD2 (the *Panzerfüsilier Regiment*), in most instances GD1 had the better, more experienced fighting force.

Anytime GD2 was engaged in battle, we always felt safest and most reassured when fighting directly alongside GD1, GD Panzer units, and any *Waffen-SS* units, especially the SS-Panzer Divisions *Das Reich* and *Totenkopf*. We felt uneasy anytime we knew foreign troops such as Romanians, Hungarians, or Italians were fighting next to us. The same was true for some units of the regular *Wehrmacht,* including several infantry divisions.

The only times we felt truly confident was when we knew that another GD unit or *Waffen-SS* unit was fighting next to us. If we knew we were next to a regular infantry division, we were scared. We called them *"Haufen,"* the heap, less cohesive and more likely to flee when heavily challenged.

On the other hand, regular troops often viewed us with jealousy and suspicion, because of our better and newer weapons, our better kept uniforms, and so on. They would call us pigs, who would in the end also die like them. They also would tell us, "You can easily look down on us, because you know you fight for a while, and then you will be pulled out to fight somewhere else. We will be stuck until we are overrun again."

It was hard to be humble when we looked at the quality of our leaders, too. Even before we arrived at the front, we had all heard about the battlefield heroics of the former commander of our regiment. *Oberst* Eugen Garski, who was killed in action near Rzhev while we were still in training in Cottbus, had earned the Knight's Cross while commanding a GD battalion in France in the spring of 1940. He was posthumously promoted to *Generalmajor*.

Our regimental commander, Oberst Horst Niemack, earned the Swords to his Knight's Cross while leading us in heavy combat in Latvia during the summer of 1944. He spoke to me once briefly. During the conversation he said, "You are from Vienna, aren't you! What a wonderful city. Now you know what you are fighting for, and why we must win." How many regimental commanders—in *any* unit of *any* army—knew the home towns of their machine gunners, or took the time to talk with them individually about what the war was about?

Our battalion commander was Major von Basse, another who earned the Knight's Cross while leading us. He was always with us; we all saw his strong, kind face in our midst when the fighting was the worst. Consequently, we all trusted him with our lives. He was killed in action during the last few weeks of the war, and posthumously promoted to *Oberstleutnant*.

The commander of our panzer regiment, *Graf* von Strachwitz, was simply a hero's hero. Wherever there was trouble, Strachwitz and his men were there. I saw him a few times in 1943, when he and elements of his regiment were supporting our operations, or at least passing through our area of operations. Although dignified, he appeared to be down to earth; there was none of the haughtiness that was often displayed by other nobles. He, also, was often to be seen at the forefront of battle when things were hottest. We all thought highly of this especially courageous officer, and were proud to be in the same division.

Other famous GD commanders included Oberst Willi Langkeit, who commanded our panzer regiment in 1944, held the Knight's Cross with Oakleaves; we knew him to be a charming man with a good sense of humor. Another was Oberst Karl Lorenz, who earned his Knight's Cross while commanding our combat engineer battalion in 1943, and later received the Oakleaves while commanding GD1. He commanded the division from September 1944 to the end of the war. His reputation, known throughout our entire division, was that of a calm, yet charismatic leader who kept his wits about him during the hottest fighting.

Of course, perhaps the most famous of all of our leaders was Hasso von Manteuffel. We all looked up to this commander, and knew him to be a highly experienced, highly competent, indeed gifted, panzer officer.

With higher ranking leaders such as these, and first-line leaders like Poldi Poschusta, there was no doubt in our minds that we were well led. Between the especially hard training at Cottbus, the excellent equipment and supplies, and, of course, our cuff title and unit heritage, there was no doubt that we were part of something special indeed. Of course, much is expected from such organizations.

Oberst Karl Lorenz, holder of the Knight's Cross with Oakleaves, who commanded a battalion and regiment in GD before succeeding to command the Division, 1944-45. (National Archives)

Bessarabia, 1944

GD was part of the German forces that retreated west from Kirovograd into Romanian territory. The Germans solidified their front in Bessarabia (today known as Moldavia), the plains immediately east of the Carpathian Mountains. GD fought to the west of Jassy (Iasi), around Targul Frumos during April and May 1944, usually alongside yTotenkopf. These battles were GD's most successful in many months, and while GD sustained heavy casualties, far more were inflicted on the Soviets.

It was after the early May fighting that Novotny's battalion was withdrawn to reequip with armored halftracks. The 1st Battalion of the Grenadier Regiment had been supplied with them since the beginning of 1943, and it was normal in German Army and Waffen-SS Panzer Divisions for a single battalion of infantry to ride in these vehicles. GD was the only German armored division besides the elite Panzerlehr Division, also considered an elite unit, to have more than one battalion equipped with these vehicles. No Waffen-SS division had more than one halftrack-borne panzergrenadier battalion.

Fred Novotny remembers . . .

The year moved on and there were more battles. Snow gave way to mud. The Russians attacked, attacked, attacked. They had thousands of tanks, artillery pieces, airplanes. Where did they all come from? According to our propaganda, we had wiped out the Russian Army in 1941, 1942, and 1943, but on they came. There was the disastrous tank battle around Targul Frumos in Romania. We fought knee-deep in mud and lost staggering quantities of men and materiel. Our counterattacks brought only temporary success, for the Russians were masters at laying mines the moment they occupied an area.

Going into the battle of Kursk the previous summer, we had still been very confident that our tanks would be superior to those of the Russians. We were confident that together with our neighbors, GD1 and the Panzer Regiment GD, we would be driving the Russians back. Even after GD lost a lot of tanks, Panthers in particular, we did not acknowledge the strength of the Russians, but blamed everything on the weather.

Going into the Bessarabian fighting in 1944, it seemed that even with the defeat at Kursk, there was always plenty of tank support from our GD Panzer units. The defeat at the Kursk-Oboyan area was actually never much of a problem to our morale. Somehow the perception among the foot soldiers was that of an organized retreat, all planned by the OKW.

About this time, it was alleged that GD commander Hoernlein should have said, "Is GD the only division on the front?" though I never heard this myself. He was replaced by the aristocrat Hasso von Manteuffel. Down at my level, Hoernlein's departure from command did not have any effect, bad or good. However the arrival and subsequent assumption of command of GD by von Manteuffel had a great morale boosting effect.

Manteuffel was built up and presented to us in orders and rumors to be the best field commander in the German Army. Everything he did was more precise and effective; whether true or not, it felt that way to us *Landsers*. We knew that Manteuffel was a physically small man with a great reputation as a leader of soldiers. The fact that *General* Hoernlein was an infantry officer, and von Manteuffel was a commander of armored forces, was not known to me, and frankly, I personally did not notice any difference in the performance of tactical operations. As far as their commanding skills, I only know that under von Manteuffel we felt stronger, more cohesive, and more important to the war effort.

At the time von Manteuffel presented me with the Iron Cross Second Class, I received a very strong handshake and a few encouraging words from what I considered a great leader. We had been on a reconnaissance patrol and were reconnoitering an entrenched Russian position. Suddenly, we became engaged in a firefight with the well-dug in Russians, at very close range. We had fixed bayonets and been forced to deal with the enemy at close quarters, and

IM NAMEN DES FÜHRERS
VERLEIHE ICH
DEM

Gefreiten N o v o t n y ,

2./Pz. Füsilier-Regt. Grossdeutschland,

DAS
EISERNE KREUZ
2. KLASSE

Jm Felde _____, 19.April __19_44

Pz. Grenadier-Division Grossdeutschland

(DIENSTSIEGEL)

Generalleutnant und Divisionskommandeur

(DIENSTGRAD UND DIENSTSTELLUNG)

The award certificate for Fred Novotny's Iron Cross 2d Class, presented "In the field" in Romania on 19 April 1944. It is signed by Panzergrenadier Division *Grossdeutschland*'s commander, Major-General (2-star, known as "*Generalleutnant*" in the *Wehrmacht*) Hasso von Manteuffel.

even hand-to-hand. It was not at all an unusual event, but I was grateful that my superiors felt that it was worthy of recognition with a decoration. Coming from the hand of von

Hasso von Manteuffel, one of the great panzer commanders of the war, shown here giving commands from a halftrack while in command of GD. Note the GD cuff title on the right sleeve. (National Archives)

Manteuffel, who we considered to be a soldier's soldier, it was an especially meaningful award. I still remember him well.

R & R in the Middle of the War

Oberleutnant Klaus Fuchs, my company commander at the time, was very intrigued with Vienna and the hotel business. He was from Kiel, Germany, on the coast of the Baltic. He spoke with me often, we talked foods of the world, and so on. While we between transfers to another battlefield, he asked me if I wood like to see his home and parents. Obviously, I said yes. We had two and a half days, over the course of a weekend.

I remember his home at the Rosenthaler See. His parents were very gracious and kind to me. I remember a great breakfast of eggs, ham, Braunschweiger, cheese, fruits, and great breads. His father was a well-known school administrator. I do not know if *Oberleutnant* Fuchs survived the war.

However, I often think of my two best days in WWII, which were spent with this caring officer at his home far from the front.

Thoughts on 20 July 1944

The events of 20 July 1944 are well known. A group of monarchist and anti-Nazi Army officers tried to assassinate Hitler and take over the German government. Their attempt failed when Hitler survived a bomb explosion at his military headquarters Rastenburg, East Prussia, and the Grossdeutschland *guard battalion at Berlin refused to support the coup. The battalion was commanded by Otto-Ernst Remer, who had earned the Knight's Cross and then the Oakleaves commanding the 1st Battalion of the Grenadier Regiment GD during 1943. Remer was personally presented his Oakleaves by Adolf Hitler. Months later, when Joseph Goebbels put Remer on the phone with Hitler, Remer had no doubt to whom the voice at the other end belonged. Hitler was still alive, and he convinced the wavering Remer to crush the insurrection.*

Spaeter relates the 20 July 1944 events in Berlin in great detail. Not suprisingly, there is no mention of the events within GD at the front that day. The internal conflict must have been an embarrassment to Spaeter and other surviving officers.

Fred Novotny remembers . . .

We were fighting in Romania when the word of the *Attentat* (assassination attempt) arrived. There happened to be very little fighting that day. We were dug in for a brief stand against the Russians, who had again assembled enormous forces against us. All of a sudden, rumors flew around. "Hitler is dead, the war will be over quickly!" Then came the word that he had been assassinated! No one seemed to know anything more.

However, very shortly officers from other GD units came around, telling us that they finally had gotten rid of Hitler, that we all will go home soon, and that this was not

Germany's war, but rather Hitler's war! We had no idea what to make of it, or how to behave. From birth, we had been conditioned to show respect for our elders and for those in authority, especially our leaders; thinking on our own had never been encouraged. We were told to "stay put," as a new regime would soon be giving orders.

It was not very long until contrary rumors flew. "Hitler is not dead; wait for orders from *Oberst* Remer!" Well, the attempt failed, Hitler was alive, and a terrible vengeance was taking place! We ourselves were to witness the hanging of GD officers by Remer loyalists. In the morning, these officers had been going around telling us things would be different, and different they were; later that day, they were hanging from quickly-erected gallows.

These were horrible times during already horrible times. Many of the hanged officers were aristocrats, and many of them believed in a greater Germany and a great German victory, but they had no love for Hitler. Now such beliefs had gotten them killed.

On to Lithuania

Memel is on the Lithuanian Baltic coast, and today is known by its Lithuanian name of Klaipeda. From its time as a Hanseatic trading city, Memel was populated by Germans, and it became a part of the German Reich during 1939. In 1945, the city returned to Lithuanian control, and the German population was expelled.

Vilkovishken was the Lithuanian name for a town on the Lithuanian side of the East Prussian border, inland from Memel. It was often referred to by Germans as Wolfsburg. The town was a regional road and rail junction, which made it vital during August 1944.

The Soviet BAGRATION offensive, launched on 22 June 1944, the third anniversary of the German invasion of the USSR, destroyed the German Army Group Center by mid-July. The front line was advanced to the Vistula River in central Poland, but the Germans retained control of the Baltic coast to the north and northeast. The Soviets briefly cut communications between East Prussia and the forces of Army Group North in Latvia and Estonia, but weak contact was restablished by vigrorous German counterattacks. The fighting at this time by GD in the Vilkovishken area prevented a rapid Soviet thrust along the shortest line to the Baltic coast, and enabled the units of Army Group North to make orderly withdrawals toward Riga and Kurland.

Novotny was not fond of his battalion's halftracks, but they were the best of their kind in the world at this time. The armored vehicles of the SdKfz 250 and 251 series allowed infantry to cooperate with tank forces to an unprecedented degree. The infantry received both a measure of protection against small arms and shrapnel, and mobility far in excess of what trucks could provide. By mid-1943, infantry riding in halftracks were an integral part of German offensive and counteroffensive operations, fighting alongside tanks and armored artillery in combined arms combat groups.

"Moving coffins" is a damning nickname, but it was far from unique to Novotny and his comrades. It was used by several armies during the war to describe vehicles which could be easily destroyed by armor-piercing weapons. Perhaps the best known example remains the Italian M13/40 tanks, which were considered deficient by the German, British and Italian forces in North Africa between 1940 and 1943.

The World War II German military exploited the widespread use of hollow-charge weapons to defeat armor. These were originally developed for mining, and worked by concentrating a jet of flame into a very small area, with sufficient force to penetrate several inches of rock or steel. A hollow charge was simple and cheap to manufacture, unlike conventional weapons whose projectiles worked through kinetic energy. By 1941, the German military recognized that the practical limit in increasing bore diameter and barrel length was within sight. Hollow charges were already in use in hand-placed versions, mainly by combat engineers for destroying fortified positions. Simple rockets were developed for delivering hollow charges to a target from a distance, and during 1943, a rocket version entered field testing as the Panzerfaust (mailed fist). Due to its success, it was widely distributed by the spring of 1944.

The Panzerfaust consisted of a disposable tube from which a short-range rocket with a hollow charge warhead was fired. It was aimed at its target through simple sights. On the early model, the range was only 30 meters at most, but this was steadily increased; during the final weeks of the war, a few of the final model were encountered, which had a range of 150 meters. In all cases, a jet of flame shot out the back of the tube at discharge, and this was potentially deadly to anyone directly behind the user, and to the user himself if in a confined area.

Even with this limitation, the Panzerfaust was tremendously effective when it did hit its target, and any tank in the world could be knocked out so long as the mass of the turret or hull was struck. Since the weapon was so simple, it could be used by anyone who received brief training and had the courage to use it. Though buildings could be hit and damaged, the usual target was an armored vehicle, and thousands were destroyed by Panzerfäuste during the war. Allied soldiers recognized its effectiveness, and used any captured ones they could find.

The United States Army also realized the possibilities of the hollow charge, and developed a launcher to fire small rockets against enemy armor. This weapon became known as a "bazooka" and German forces captured some in Tunisia late in 1942. These were studied and replicated into a larger diameter German version, which was also in wide use by 1944, though in far smaller numbers than the Panzerfaust. The German bazooka was nicknamed in Landser slang the Panzerschreck (tank terror) or more often, the Ofenrohr (stovepipe).

Destroying an enemy tank with any of these hollow-charge weapons required a great deal of courage, since the attacker was normally exposed to return fire (and sometimes had to physically place the charge on the tank). In the German armed forces, success in this enterprise was recognized, from early 1942, with the award of a distinctive badge sewn on the upper right sleeve. Men who wore these tank destruction badges received a great deal of respect, and those with multiple awards were regarded with a measure of awe. The known record for tanks destroyed was held by Günther Viezenz, a platoon and company commander, and later battalion leader in the 252d Infantry Division. Viezenz was credited with twenty-one destroyed tanks, and survived the war to later enjoy a successful career in the Bundeswehr.

Fred Novotny remembers . . .

In late May 1944, we were taken out of the front lines to be reorganized. By August, we were ready to be shipped to northeastern Germany and the Baltics; destination: Memel, a major city on the rim of what was then East Prussia.

We were still proud to be part of our unit, now the 1st Battalion, *Panzerfüsilier Regiment Grossdeutschland*. However, we were very wary of our halftracks. We called them "moving coffins." The speed was great, as was the weaponry, but the armor was no match for the cannon on the T-34, the Russians' excellent tank. In battle, we would rather walk behind or ahead of our halftrack than be in it. A great number were lost.

By this time, Major von Basse was our battalion commander. We were told how lucky we were as fusiliers to have a man with such war experience to lead us. He personally talked to us on many occasions, moving up to our foxholes or joining us when we were fighting, giving us encouraging words of advice. He was an officer of real stature, and we completely trusted this man. We were sure most all of his

A moment of quiet before an attack, Summer 1944. This is a SdKFz 251 armored halftrack, in the final "D" version introduced in the spring of 1944.

Another view of a D model SdKFz 251 during the summer of 1944. Fred Novotny sits on the vehicle with his legs visible. While these halftracks were advanced for their time, Novotny held a poor opinion of them, as they were easily penetrated by armor-piercing rounds. Still, they provided the best possible means for infantry to accompany tanks during armored attacks.

decisions would be made with our welfare in mind. As I mentioned before, I certainly looked up to him.

The Russians opened with a massive operation called BAGRATION. We fought major battles in Tauroggen, Virballen, Vilkovishken, and Memel. The Russian armies were relentless, however, and we fell back. One day, we were making a stand at a road running to a wooded area. I was in a foxhole near a wall outside of a cemetery. I was again using an MG42. The next foxhole was twenty feet away. I was facing the opening in the woods into which the road ran, where two anti-tank German guns, were located on each side of me.

Through the woods, we could hear the growling of Russian tanks on the move. The noise grew louder and louder. My heart was pounding. Somehow, I was afraid this would be my last battle.

Now, we could see the first Russian tanks roaring out of the woods, guns blasting; our antitank guns, in turn, started shooting back with all they had. The tanks kept coming. These were heavily-armored Stalin tanks, the largest the Russians had at the time. The lead tank was hit by an antitank gun round and started burning. Other tanks simply pushed it aside and kept on coming. They were very near. I fixed the

Beglei tel für

Verwundete

u. andere chirurgisch zu Behandelnde.

Nichttransportfähig:	**zwei** rote Streifen
Transportfähig:	**ein** roter Streifen
Marschfähig:	**kein** roter Streifen

Name: *Novotny*

Dienstgrad: *Gefr.*

Truppenteil: *2. / F R S D.*

Verletzung:

Gehirn in dui Ruin,

Knochenverletzung?
Sonstiges Leiden:

Erhielt an stark wirkenden Arzneien		
innerlich ?	Gabe	Zeit
Eingespritzt ?		
Wundstarrkrampfserum ?		

Another tag from an injury on 18 October 1944, when Novotny received a concussion.

closest tank in my *Panzerfaust* sights, closed my eyes with fear, and fired. The next thing I knew, I woke up in a field hospital. I was told the same moment I hit and stopped the tank, a round from the Stalin's main gun had hit the wall above my head, and shrapnel wounds and a concussion from falling stones had knocked me unconscious. The next morning, a lieutenant came and placed a *Panzerknack Abzeichen*, a tank-kill medallion, on my chest. Once again, someone above had looked out for me.

Our most common infantry anti-tank weapon at the time was the *Panzerfaust*. Also in use, but never by me, was the *"Ofenrohr"* bazooka. However, the most-used weapon was the *"Haftmine"* (hollow-charge magnetic mine), which had to be physically attached by soldiers to the target. These were very effective. They were the cause of many a tank's demise, but were also the source of the deaths of many brave men.

I received my tank destruction badge in the field hospital outside Memel. Later in the war, I was occasionally asked what I had to do to receive the badge, and how I did it. I was just lucky to survive to get it!

Love in Wartime

A "love in war" story comes to mind. The object of my affection was a girl named Grete. After receiving light wounds in knocking out the tank, I was pulled out of my unit and shipped back to Kutno, Poland to recuperate for a short time. Three days after my arrival, I was ordered to report to a shop that sold wild game. The owner was a stern man, a member of the Party, as I could see from the emblem in his lapel. The store belonged to Polish people before Poland was defeated; this was surely not unusual. I no longer know the owner's name.

He had a young lady in a *Luftwaffe* uniform helping him out; she did paperwork chores for him besides her military duties. This store owner must have had the right connections to the upper echelons. As I found out, Grete was twenty. I was barely nineteen. We fell in love instantly. She had a one-room flat at sidewalk level, with a single bed, one small table, two chairs, one small cupboard, and a pot-bellied stove with a twelve-inch surface on top for cooking. The toilet and a cold water faucet were outside on a corridor. On my second day there, I was invited to share her "paradise."

At work at the store, I learned how to skin deer and hares, pluck feathers from ducks, and so on. I also was counter clerk, and a salesman, all in all a cushy set up during a harsh wartime. Ninety-nine percent of our customers were Germans—clerks, doctors, city administrators, and bureaucrats only. The hard work was done by the Polish people.

Grete and I would eye each other all day. We could not wait to get to her flat, make love, and talk and dream of a life after the war all night long. She was from a small town near Heidelberg.

Soon, I was ordered to report back to my outfit. We were both sad and shocked that this episode in our lives had to end so soon. The next day at 0500, with tears in my eyes, I had to board the train. Grete stood on the platform, her eyes as wet as mine. We never saw or heard from each other again.

With the *Führer* Grenadier Division

Grossdeutschland *was the parent formation for the the* Führer Begleit Bataillon, *Hitler's "escort" battalion that helped to guard his headquarters in East Prussia. Elements of the battalion were often detached for frontline duty, both to give them experience and to provide commanders in critical sectors of the front with a small, well-armed, elite force for counterattacks. Meanwhile, disaster overcame the German fronts in France and Belorussia. New independent armored units, known as Panzer Brigades, were formed to help quickly shore up the front in the crisis zones. Grossdeutschland and its guard and training elements played a part in this, with the* Führer *Escort Battalion increased to brigade size. A new sister unit was created, and named the* Führer *Grenadier Brigade. Both were combined arms formations with integral armor, infantry, and artillery battalions. In early 1945, after seeing heavy combat in the Ardennes Offensive (the "Battle of the Bulge"), the two brigades were raised to nominal divisional status, although they were never manned or equipped commensurately.*

The Führer *Grenadier Division (FGD) was commanded by Oakleaves holder Hellmuth Mäder. It fought in Pomerania during the mid-February 1945, in the* SONNENWENDE *(SOLSTICE) offensive that liberated Arneswalde. It then fought in the counterattack around Lauban in Silesia, the last successful German offensive action of the war.*

Novotny was not yet a member of the division at this time. He was in Guben with the GD replacement and training units. The 3d Battalion of the Panzergrenadier Ersatz und Ausbildung *Regiment GD formed the core of the defense of the city, which began on 13 February 1945. This battalion fought at Guben until mid-March, before being assigned to reinforce the numerically weak FGD (which had only 4,229 men on 27 January 1945, far below true divisional strength). It was then sent to Vienna where it joined FGD as the 2d Battalion of the unusually titled* Panzer Radfahr Regiment Sommer *(Armored Bicycle Regiment commanded by Major Sommer, with "Armored" being an honorific to reflect its service with an armored division). This title was soon changed to the equally cumbersome* Führer Panzergrenadier Regiment FGD 2.

Novotny become a member of FGD in late March, and his unit finally abandoned Vienna during the night of 12/13 April. New positions were established to the north, in the Korneuburg area. These were held, despite sometimes fierce fighting, until the end of the war.

Fred Novotny remembers . . .

Now an incredible turn of fate befell me. After my three weeks recuperation, I left the hospital with orders to report to a detached element of *Grossdeutchland*. I could tell that everyone was very uneasy, but the words were never spoken. We had lost the war. Everybody knew, but nobody mentioned it. Only people who have lived under a dictatorship will understand how and why this could be.

I was assigned to a new division under General Mäder. We fought east of Berlin, in the Guben area, in early 1945. A brief episode, another incident of "love in war," sticks with me, for its sheer insanity. It obviously sprang from the fear young people have of dying before they can experience "life," which is to say "love."

During the intense house-to-house battle in Guben, we were told we would be withdrawn during the night, to be shipped to another sector where the Russians had just broken through. I was assigned to be the rearguard, some fifty meters behind my group. We were moving inside rowhouses, through holes we punched through the walls, from one home to the next.

All of a sudden, the unusual site of a young woman of undetermined age (because of the ragged clothing and lack of grooming) came slowly up the cellar stairs. I was puzzled to see her and said, "what in the hell are you doing here? This is a war zone, and a very dangerous one at that!" There was constant mortar and machine-gun fire coming from God knows where, it was surely not a safe place to be.

She told me, tears running down her cheeks, that she was too late when the last people fled, and had decided to hide underground to wait out the battle. I asked her if she had food and water, and she said she did. At the end of this short conversation, we looked at each other, then took each others' hands. Not a word was spoken, as we must have had the same thought: we might be dead tomorrow.

Suddenly, we were lying on the floor, fumbling wildly, furiously making love, without a word. The shooting outside never stopped, but we never heard it. I got up, kissed her, and she disappeared back into the cellars. I moved on. We were two young people afraid to die. I often wondered if she survived the war, and/or the horrible peace that followed?

As I think about this episode in a time where life was not worth a nickel, I smile when I try to picture the situation many years later. Two terrified, yet overheated young people, hormones raging, my steel helmet bouncing on my head, my battle gear tangling and getting in the way (gas-mask, mess kit, spade, and two hand grenades in my belt). How this lovemaking worked is a puzzle to me today. Desperation and the life instinct are powerful forces indeed.

I caught up with my unit, and straightaway, we were transported to Austria, my homeland. I began to have high hopes. I would see my family again. I could not believe it.

We arrived at Korneuburg, near Vienna, and I was incredulous that destiny had sent me back home to take a last stand against the Russians. We were optimisitc that after a fight here we would be able to surrender to the Americans. Rumors circulated that the Americans would treat us well. Our commanding general let it be known he would try to capitulate to the Americans when the time came. We had heard horrible things about what happened to soldiers captured by the Russians.

The situation was almost hopeless. It was 30 March 1945, and we were digging in around Aspern Air Field, outside of Vienna. My thoughts were constantly with my mother, father and two sisters. I even contemplated going AWOL, but there was an awful reality: Deserters everywhere were being shot by their own officers. We had heard of the case of the seventeen-year-old soldier who had found a bike. He was pushing it and was shot in the head because his officers thought he might be deserting.

I was not yet twenty-one at the time. I was promoted to *Obergefreiter*, and that left me the highest ranking one left in a group of two hundred. There were no officers, no sergeants. They all had been killed or wounded within the last twenty-four hours.

On the next day, a young man of twenty-four, a sergeant, was made company commander. He came from another group. The only officers we saw were SS officers, and very few of these. They were not there to direct fighting, just to enforce discipline so the army would not totally disintegrate. Their techniques were draconian, to say the least.

I was given charge of twelve boys, none of them over sixteen. Everyone was talking or thinking of running off, but very few did. The possibility of being caught and shot was too great. At the time, I had not slept for thirty-six hours, having marched day and night. I was reeling with fatigue. I took these boys to the area where they were supposed to dig foxholes and defend. They were clearly afraid. Then, I must have fallen asleep after I took the last of them to their positions. I woke up cold and shivering, with a gun at my head. It was not a Russian, but rather a young German *SS* officer screaming at me that I should be shot. I discovered that all twelve kids had left their positions and disappeared, leaving a hole in our defensive position. The only reason I am still here is that the officer I was taken to was my former drill sergeant from Cottbus, and he remembered me. He looked at my combat decorations, slapped me on the back, and told the young officer to leave me alone. Again, I had made it through. To think that I had survived the war in Russia and come so close to being shot by a crazed member of my own side!

---

1 April 1945. My twenty-first birthday. I thought of so many of Europe's youth that were dead, or crippled, and there I was, twenty-one, and so close to home. Willy, one of the other old soldiers (he was twenty-two) celebrated with me. We found a basket with forty eggs on a farm. We scrambled them all and ate until we were sick. What a celebration! We had no bread, just the eggs, and lots of water.

Somewhere near Vienna, 1 April 1945. So close to home and still so far away from family. Fred Novotny, at right, as a member of the *Führer* Grenadier Division on his twenty-first birthday.

Vienna, Austria, 1928. The cousins: Ossi, who became mayor of Springfield, Illinois, before retiring; Edith; Fred Novotny; and his sister, Jutta, who now lives in Peoria, Illinois.

Vienna, 1930. *Lehrer* Lenz (Teacher Lenz) and his first grade class. Novotny is in the second row, third from right.

First-grade classmates at their only meeting, Vienna, 1943, during
the height of the war. Novotny stands at top right.

Fourteen-year-old Fred Novotny, second from right, on his first
day as an apprentice at the Kahlenberg restaurant, Vienna, 1938.

Fred Novotny's drawing of the Kahlenberg Restaurant in the Vienna woods, while a prisoner at Camp Georgia, Russia, in 1946. Done from memory.

Erich Taussig was Fred Novotny's fellow apprentice at the Kahlenberg. As he was three years older, Taussig was drafted sooner, and assigned to the *Luftwaffe*. He sent this photo to Novotny from the Netherlands during the spring of 1941. Taussig survived the war, and passed away during the 1990s.

Two members of Fred Novotny's RAD battalion stand guard outside the La Godinier Seminary in France during 1942.

Fred Novotny's RAD battalion marched toward St. Nazaire to counter the British Commando landing, 28 March 1942.

A tired Fred Novotny sits shirtless at left, eating lunch between construction assignments with the RAD during 1942.

This blurred
photo shows Fred
Novotny standing
guard duty dur-
ing his 1942 RAD
service.

The 2d Company of the *Panzerfüsilier Regiment* joins Ukrainian
civilians for an Easter celebration during the spring of 1943. It is
noteworthy that the crowd includes women, children, and old
men but no younger men. These were all away, fighting with the
Soviet or German forces, or hiding with partisan bands.

The only thing he brought home with him: Novotny's self-engraved mess kit, still in his possession. Engraved on it are the towns, dates, and events during his imprisonment in Russia.

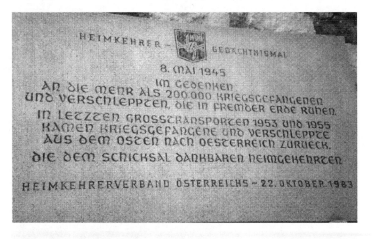

HEIMKEHRER – GEDÄCHTNISMAL

8. MAI 1945

IM GEDENKEN
AN DIE MEHR ALS 200.000 KRIEGSGEFANGENEN
UND VERSCHLEPPTEN, DIE IN FREMDER ERDE RUHEN.
IN LETZTEN GROSSTRANSPORTEN 1953 UND 1955
KAMEN KRIEGSGEFANGENE UND VERSCHLEPPTE
AUS DEM OSTEN NACH OESTERREICH ZURUECK.
DIE DEM SCHICKSAL DANKBAREN HEIMGEKEHRTEN

HEIMKEHRERVERBAND ÖSTERREICHS – 22. OKTOBER 1983

This monument stands at Leopoldsburg in the Vienna Woods. It offers the thanks and of the Austrian people to Austrian prisoners of war who returned from captivity after years of suffering, and remembers those who rest forever in foreign soil. This photo was shot by Novotny's American friend, William Wilsen, the retired Conductor of the Peoria Symphony Orchestra.

Kahlenberg Restaurant, Vienna, 1949. Fred Novotny, seated on right, with colleagues.

Kahlenberg
Restaurant, Vienna,
Fall 1948. Fred
Novotny, left, with
his friend Vic, both
home from impris-
onment in Russia.
Vic died in 1993 in
Detroit, Michigan.

Seven survivors of Tkvibuli held a reunion in Vienna in the early 1990s. Fred Novonty was unable to attend, but later received this photo of the event. The men include Wospiel, Hörner, Kotek, and Klanzelmeyer.

Retired *Unteroffiziere* Karl Otto and his wife at a reunion in Mannheim, Germany, during 1987. It was Otto who forced Fred Novotny to keep marching during one partic- ularly difficult moment in the retreat from Ukraine. Novotny believes that Otto's action saved his life.

3

Communist Captivity

The Vienna-Tkvibuli Express

According to Spaeter's GD history, Mäder was able to surrender the FGD to American forces on 9 May 1945. A few small elements were moved west, and became American prisoners, but the bulk of the division was turned over to the Soviets without warning on the morning of 13 May. The Americans and Soviets had agreed that the German soldiers of units which fought exclusively against the Soviets were to be turned over without exception.

Novotny was indeed close to home, but evading Soviet captivity at this time would likely have done little good. Had he gone into American captivity and been eventually released, or evaded all capture, once he returned to Vienna, he likely would have been taken into Soviet captivity. This happened to thousands of German soldiers who were released by the Americans and returned to their homes in the Soviet zone of occupation. Had this occurred to Novotny, his fate in the Gulag could possibly have been worse than what he lived through!

In a sense, Novotny and the FGD were lucky to enter Soviet captivity. The next day, 14 May, the survivors of the SS-Totenkopf Division (the old comrades of Novotny and other GD veterans) were turned over to Soviet forces near Pregarten.

Fred Novotny remembers . . .

4 May 1945. We were to assemble in a meadow near Pregarten, not far from Vienna. Rumors raced through the troops that our commanding general had made a secret deal with the Americans to take us prisoner. There were about nine thousand of us and we were to stay put in order to get papers from the Americans so we would not be captured by the Russians. I could not believe that the war was ending and that I was still alive and very close to home. Thank God, I thought.

We were circled by American tanks in the pasture and only the soldiers in the periphery of our encampment had any contact with the *Amis,* as we called the Americans. We felt secure. A few among us knew better, however, and they went AWOL. Others among us said to one another, "Let's just take off." There were very few guards and they didn't seem to care. The Russians had many more troops than the *Amis,* said those in favor of leaving. How right they were.

On the morning of 7 May, we awoke to find the number of tanks surrounding us had increased greatly, and that they belonged to the Russians. During the night, they had changed guards and now we were Russian prisoners. We were scared and shocked. My indecisiveness to simply take off cost me many months of my young life, for those who fled did not suffer through those awful Russian prison camps.

The next morning, we were still surrounded by Russian tanks and screaming soldiers dressed in brown earth-tone uniforms. *"Davai, davai"* ("move, move") they screamed at us. That was all we heard all that day. We were herded to the town of Zwettl, into a camp, which appeared to have housed Allied or Russian prisoners. There were high wire fences and the crudest sort of huts. We were standing in long columns waiting endlessly to enter the camp. The word got around that the Russian soldiers were moving among us and taking rings, watches . . . everything of value they could find. You could hide your valuables temporarily, but only until the searching began in earnest inside the camp. I had a watch-band of the kind that slipped through and under the bottom of the watch, so I quickly slid the watch off the band and put the band on again.

Soon I was approached by two young Mongolian soldiers saying *"Chassi, chassi"* (which means watch), "give me, give me the watch." I let them see only the part of the watchband visible under my sleeve. I pretended not to want to lose my watch, so I held my wrist and said, "*Mein, mine, chassi mein.*" After a while, one of the Russians got mad, pushed up my sleeve to pull off the watch and saw that it was a band only.

Lager Zwettl. A sketch made two years later.

For this, one of them smashed his rifle butt into my mouth and again into my back. Such was my first encounter with our Russian captors, even before I was in the camp.

When we finally entered the camp grounds, we were counted and moved into barracks, where we collapsed onto the floor and fell asleep. Early the next morning, at 0500, a Russian officer who spoke German came into the room. "During the day," he said, "there will be a time set aside for showers, disinfection, and delousing. In the meantime, go outside and there will be black coffee and black bread from the field kitchen." So far, so good.

I still had the equivalent, in *Reichsmarks*, of about two thousand dollars I had won from nonstop playing of black-jack and other card games, and the pay we received month-ly. It was stuffed into pockets and I assumed I would lose all this money rather quickly. I wanted to get word to my par-ents to let them know I was alive. We had had no contact for the past six months. There were at the time a lot of women standing around outside the wire fences, children talking to prisoners of war and the like, so I moved over to the fence and struck up a conversation with a young woman. She won-dered about what was going to happen to us, and to her. She wanted to learn what we knew about the Russians. "Will we all be raped?" she asked.

I told her to try to get away from this place as fast as she could and try to get to Vienna, where she could disappear much more easily. She seemed sincere, so I gave her my par-ents' address, my name, and asked her to please let them know I was alive, and where she had seen me. Then I gave her all the money I had and told her, "If you contact my par-ents, it is all yours and maybe it will help you start your life again." I never asked her name. Four years later, however, I discovered that she had, indeed, seen my parents, but was never seen again by any of us. She never told my parents about the money, but perhaps that was understandable.

On the evening of the seventh day of our captivity, orders were screamed at us to take all of our possessions and step outside. We were divided into groups of sixty, each group with one guard. The little Mongolian assigned to my group laughed and said to us, "Now the German pigs will all go to my country and no one will ever return." He was laughing and repeating these words again and again. What a prospect. For hundreds of thousands of prisoners, his prediction was to come true.

Russian soldiers brought two huge wooden crates and placed them in front of our group. This was being done throughout the camp. We were told to strip, put our uniforms in front of us, and dump all our jewelry, chains, and watches into one of the crates, and our medals and pictures in another. We were told to keep only our identity tags. Even our *Soldbücher*, our identification books, were collected and matched with the identity tags afterwards.

We learned quickly that everything moves at a snail's pace in Russian life. It took a long time for these simple procedures, and we were still standing, stark naked, in the sun two days later. Thank heavens it was a warm May in 1945 in that part of the world. Finally, we had to step away from everything we had owned. We were sent into the showers. After three minutes, we were herded out the other door to confront a wall of Russian women in uniforms, each with a brush in one hand, and a bucket in the other. The buckets, we discovered, were filled with kerosene and the women would brush our chests and genitals and underarms, causing our skin to burn painfully. Another woman would shave our body hair and head. It was both humiliating and dehumanizing. We looked at one another in amazement. How ugly we looked, but I think somehow we managed to laugh about ourselves, even as the Russian women laughed and made bawdy remarks about our manhood. Then we were given Russian uniforms, socks, shoes, and a very coarse blanket. From this day on, these were our only possessions. And we were reduced on this day in May to people with only names and numbers.

Now we were to begin a twenty-seven-day ride into Hell. "Up, up!" they screamed at us. It was 0400. We got dressed, grabbed our blankets, mess kits, and spoons, and lined up outside the barracks where we were split up again into groups of sixty. In these groups, we marched to the railroad

This portrait of Novotny was drawn by Franz Eidenberger with ground up bricks. The caption reads, "Prisoner of War captivity in Russia."

station as Russian soldiers kept hollering and pushing us to get into the cattle cars as quickly as possible.

So many of us were jammed into each car that there was hardly any place to stand. There was a stove in the middle, a cord of wood to use for the fire, and a four-inch hole in the floor. On each side of the cattle car were shelves spaced four-feet high, and on each side was a kerosene lamp.

Little did we know how the Russians functioned. It took a full three days before we were to leave. After a lot of jostling for space, pushing, and hollering, we were forced to settle in to these horribly cramped quarters. It was very dark. We discovered what the four-inch hole was for and we used it; it was the only "toilet" for sixty men. It soon began to stink very badly since the train was not moving and all the waste accumulated on the tracks under the cattle car.

At around 0200 on the second day, the doors were unlocked and heaved open, and a large bucket with a ladle was pushed in. This, some kind of soup we could not identify, was our first meal.

There was so much chaos, such pushing and shoving, that most of the soup was spilled. After a while, one of our men fought his way to the middle of the cattle car and announced in a loud voice, "We will all starve to death if we do not maintain discipline and divide the little food we get." It turned out that he was a lieutenant from another outfit, the only officer in our car. He assumed leadership responsibilities in our group.

On the second day, things went much better. We all stood in line to wait for our soup. Each of us also received a slice of bread. We were very restless, however, sitting for hours, days, in this dark, smelly boxcar. Rumors began to circulate about the plans the Russians had for us. Would they let us sit here and starve? What would life in a prison camp be like? Would we survive? How long did they intend to keep us? Where would they take us? Our anxiety fueled these questions and we were understandably afraid.

Other than the meal, nothing of note happened on the third day. We settled down and fell asleep. All of the sudden, sometime during the early morning hours of the third day, there was a bang and a thump and we were moving. We woke up. The prisoner who gained the top spot, on the highest shelf, was the only one with access to a opening through which he could see out. He reported to us that he saw some signs on some of the buildings we passed. We were going east. This we knew for sure.

Later on the third day, we woke up to discover that we were on a siding once again, parked outside a railroad yard. It would be twenty-four hours before we moved again. Our lookout reported that we were in Hungary.

These days passed interminably. Our muscles became stiff. There was no way to move, no room to stretch, no way to do anything but sit or sleep. Days later, our lookout reported we were in Romania. It was late in the day, but there was still light, and suddenly there was noise, hollering, running, and shooting. Our lookout reported the commotion but didn't know what it was all about. Later, we learned that three prisoners had escaped. The Russian guards simply pulled three innocent Romanians into the train, and these took the place of the three who had escaped. They did not understand what was happening to them, but the Russians needed to arrive with the number of men they had started out with when they left our camp.

We were becoming infested with lice and developed rashes. We could not wash ourselves for at least ten days. We were becoming irritated and short-tempered with one another. Thanks to Lieutenant Krager, our leader, we would talk about many different things, and he would act as a teacher to help keep our minds active.

We divided drinking water, and five men would then be able to shave and wash their faces and hands with the same water. We tried mightily to keep our humanity, our sanity.

Even so, many of our comrades did not survive. Every day, the guards would come in and look for bodies to remove. As the days and weeks passed, it became less crowded, but hardly more bearable.

At last, we arrived at Romania's port on the Black Sea, Constanza. We were weak and confused as we debarked from this awful train and were herded onto a ship named "Transylvania." It was very small and there were many of us. We were prodded and pushed inside until we were like sardines. There was standing room only. I was one of the lucky ones. A friend, a former U-boat man, told me, "Fred, we must remain on the upper deck. No matter how much shoving there is, we will hold hands, stay together and I'll see that we stay up here. Below the decks, too many people will die." How right he was.

Many of our fellow prisoners ended up two decks down, with insufficient air and space. After a full day, the ship was finally ready to sail. The waters of the Black Sea were very rough, and everyone was sick. I felt horrible and told my friend, "I will die, I will die. We've come so far and now we're going to die." He told me to shut up and to do only what he did, and not to move from our spot. He knew it was a three-day trip.

It was a horrible voyage, marked by moaning and screaming. There was no food, no water, no hygiene facilities. What we had on the train, where we thought it was the worst, seemed like paradise. At last, we arrived at the Russian Black Sea port of Novorossisk.

There were hundreds and hundreds who did not leave the ship with us. They had perished like animals deep in the bowels of this ship, without food, without water, stinking and screaming for mercy. No one cared. It was each man for himself.

What followed was an unimaginably hard three days. We formed miles of bodies, mostly skin and bones, marching up into the Caucasus Mountains in Soviet Georgia. Hundreds more did not survive this ordeal, for there was no food and only the water in the ditches next to the road. I still shudder when I think what happened to all these men, some fathers, some grandfathers, who would never return to their loved ones, but were to die in thirst, hunger and agony on some lonely Russian road. I myself felt like an old, worn-out warrior, at just twenty-one years of age. Over the years, I have tried to piece together why and how I was able to survive this terrible journey and march.

A typical outfit as worn in the Caucasus. The drawing was made by Fred Novotny during July 1945, soon after arriving at Tkvibuli.

I also found out that things can always get worse. It was seemed to be the worst of times, to be sure, but, inconceivably, much worse ones soon were in store.

Finally, we, the survivors, marched, or rather dragged, ourselves, into Tkvibuli, which was to be our home for a long time. Twenty-seven arduous days and nights and we were at the camp. It was surrounded by treeless hills with guard towers everywhere. We were herded into a large open square surrounded by wooden barracks. We were divided into groups of twelve men per room. The rooms had wooden shelves, upper and lower on both walls, and no straw, or mattress or any kind of cover on the wood. All we had was our blankets and our uniforms.

We were so tired we could hardly stand, so we fell upon our hard, wooden shelves, but the guards came into the room and ordered us all outside. We were told to undress. We went through the showers again and received the kerosene treatment again from females, but we didn't care any more. Then we were given a half liter of watery soup, three ounces of corn bread, and we were able to sleep a full ten hours. It was almost like heaven.

Camp Tkvibuli, 1945. Map of prison camp in Georgia and surrounding states and countries. Drawing by Fred Novotny.

At 0600, we were called outside. For the whole day, we would be outside. One by one, we were interrogated. Prisoners with their blood type tattooed in their armpits were separated and taken to the other part of the prison camp. These were members of the SS. We were interrogated for four solid days, always by different Russian officers.

On day five, we were told we would now have to pay for what we did to the Russian people. If we were lucky, we might be released in a few years. The news completely devastated us. Most of us, during those first few months, came to accept the probability we would never see our homes or loved ones again, so we became extremely close, almost like members of a family, and we came to live for one another.

Slowly, however, the survival instinct took over and we began to connive, to rob, and to steal just to get a few extra grams of food. Day after day, we worked in the coal mines, the *Lenin Schachti*. These mines, we were told, were 1,600 feet deep and were in poor repair. They had not been used since 1919, at which time they also were operated by German prisoners. If we were lucky, we would make it up to the top again, but our fear, before we descended into the mine for the first time, was intense and numbing. We were given old, beat-up hardhats, with lights attached, and rubber slippers, since we would be working in water all day. The mine shafts were only five feet high, so we were had to work bent over for the whole shift.

We were ordered to break loose eight tons of coal per man per shift, and when we were done, we filled the carts. Each of us had to fill eight carts and we had metal tags with our assigned number. These we attached to each cart. If it happened to be short of eight tons, a portion or all of our evening soup and bread would be withheld.

Hungry as we were, we worked ten hours a day just to get our full ration of soup. With us were Russian-born prisoners, mostly Ukranians, who had fought with General Vlasov on the German side against the Communists. They, being considered traitors, were treated worse than dogs. As it was discovered later, half of the two million who had fought under General Vlasov died in the camps.

As time went on, I sometimes thought back to the days during the war when we were stationed near Hannover, at a *Truppenübungsplatz*, or military training post. There I had seen Russians in one of our prison camps and we called them filthy pigs, or "*Untermenschen*," which means underclass or inferior people, because they were picking up pieces of food that Germans spit out or threw away. Now that I was hungry, I understood what they had gone through. The Russians in our camp were eating smelt, a tiny, sardine-like fish, out of brown paper bags, biting off the heads and spitting them out. We were so hungry, we picked them up and the Russians would call out "*Swinia*," or "swine." Well, what goes around comes around. Many years later, in America, these impressions gave me a wholly different sense of how to treat people around me. I would look at them and think back to those days at Tkvibuli, our days in the mines, and our nights in the cold, hard barracks.

———⇒●⇐———

Despite the awful treatment we received, I could never really blame the Russians completely. They were really no different from us. Even today, I have a recurring vision of the very young Russian face, red cheeks, big blue eyes staring straight into mine. It was during heavy house-to-house fighting in the city of Guben outside of Berlin. We occupied the right side of the street, the Russians the left side. It was a street of row houses. We were advancing inside the houses by breaking through walls as we went along, and the Russians were doing the same on the other side of the street. What terrible way of destroying our own people's houses.

There I was, however, dashing past a window. As I did, I caught a quick glimpse across the narrow street of this very young face peering out of a small window, gun in hand, facing me. My face could not have looked too old to him, either, for I was barely twenty. Immediately, I positioned my rifle to face him and shoot. But something strange happened to me, and it must have happened to him, too. For a few moments we stared at one another. Neither of us pulled the trigger.

Slowly, his stare metamorphosed into a smile, and mine did the same; I don't know why, but we then both waved. Each of us then disappeared into the houses on our respective sides of the street. Even today, I wonder if he survived the war, and if he might remember this strange incident. What made both of us refrain from shooting must have been a guiding hand from heaven, from our respective guardian angels.

The Camp, 1945

Novotny's stories of camp life may seem fanciful, but are often echoed in studies of the Soviet concentration camp system. The accounts collected by Solzhenitsyn for The Gulag Archipelago *are, if anything, often more horrific. Novotny was fortunate to not serve in a colder climate, and also to avoid the still more brutal treatment given to SS men and Soviet collaborators. It is a wonder that he kept his humanity and his sanity.*

Fred Novotny remembers . . .

Kapetan Frankfurter was an NKVD officer and also a doctor of medicine for our camp, and he had an incredibly sadistic streak. He would call us into his office where he had a dentist chair and some equipment. It was all very crude, with a manual drill operated by a wooden foot pedal. He would tell we needed dental care, would drill holes into perfectly good teeth, then fill them. After this painful procedure, without novocaine, he would then pull the teeth he had just finished drilling.

You could hear the screaming all day from his "office." One day it was my turn. I was very scared. I entered his room, where, in four days, I had seven teeth drilled and then pulled. I have never been able to forget the pain and even to this day, I am reluctant to go to the dentist.

As bad as this was, perhaps the worst torment was the nagging, endless hunger that afflicted us all. As you can well understand, food was very scarce in Russia after the war, and it naturally was much worse in the prison camps. What we were given, we discovered later, was scientifically calculated to keep us alive—barely.

These were the typical daily portions: at 0500, we were served eight ounces of black coffee of indescribably bitter flavor, with no sugar or milk; 100 grams, or about 3.5 ounces of hot, soggy cornbread, which amounted to about one bite. We were allowed five minutes for this breakfast.

At noon, we got our "soup," which consisted of eight ounces of hot, tasteless water with millet kernels. There was no salt, no fat, no greens. At dinner, served in the early

An impression of a Soviet prison camp by artist Franz Eidenberger. Notice the words "Lager Tkibuli [sic] Georgien" in the lower-left corner.

evening when we returned from work, we had eight ounces of coffee and 100 grams of cornbread. We understood the life-sustaining qualities were in the millet.

We came to the conclusion that if we let the bread dry out, which would make it somehow like toast, it would take us longer to chew and therefore make us seem less hungry. Hungry was the word, however, that accompanied us, night and day. So, sometimes we would not eat the bread, but rather keep it until noon, sitting there in the sun guarding our precious pieces of bread so that it would dry. Hunger left little honor and one would steal one's neighbor's bread in the blink of an eye. We would wrap this dry piece of bread in a not-so-clean rag and keep it with us. The idea that we still had some bread while others had eaten theirs made us feel as if we had more to eat.

One scene I still recall is sitting outside at the camp, legs apart, and the sun shining on a tiny piece of bread, the prisoners' way of making toast. Once this toast was ready, we would chew every tiny morsel as long as possible. It seemed, for a time, to still our constant hunger.

Since our thoughts were always on food, some fellows would come up with the craziest ideas about how to supplement our meager rations. Some of these included tree or bush leaves soaked in the coffee and tree bark added to the soup, which may have hurt rather than helped since we were constantly suffering from severe diarrhea.

Some prisoners occasionally were lucky and got jobs in the woods. They were able to bring back berries, wild green apples, or plums. Three cherry-sized apples could be traded for a pair of shoes, which meant that some prisoners went barefooted just to get a few apples. Eight berries were worth a pair of gloves.

Only twice in all the prison months did we actually receive the rations we should have been getting according to the Geneva Convention. Twice, high-ranking officers from Moscow were expected and the guards and officers got busy cleaning us up, cleaning out the quarters, and giving us an unbelievable feast. It consisted of eight ounces of coffee and the same amount of milk, 200 grams of bread and 40 grams of butter for breakfast, twelve ounces of soup with four ounces of meat and vegetables for lunch, and eight ounces of coffee and milk, 200 grams of bread, and an apple for dinner.

While we were supposed to be getting this every day, it was actually being diverted to the black market and to the Russian guards and officers. We also found out that hundreds of Red Cross and family packages were never given to us. You had this treatment coming, the Russian guards would tell us, because you destroyed our country.

Although worse off in our hunger than the general population, we were not alone. The total lack of a transportation system meant that Georgian oranges, grapes, and corn would simply rot. There was no way to get such produce to the people. If they were not consumed where they grew, they simply spoiled.

The Grim Day-to-Day

The corruption of the Soviet system was legendary. And the USSR had never signed the Geneva convention, so there was no hesitation in diverting material and goods intended for the camps into the black market.

Fred Novotny remembers . . .

At the camp, days and days passed with no change in our routine. They were boring and endless. There were constant rumors that we were to be shipped off to Siberia, or shot, or sent home, or given extra food. We went to work in the mornings, did our jobs, were marched back at night, washed with cold water, and collapsed onto our wooden shelves. There was never hot water, so we were unable to wash away the coal dust and grime which built up day after day. We would get all sorts of eczemas, rashes, and other skin irritations for which there was no medicine and no cure. Our ultimate goal was simply survival.

One of the most treasured items we could acquire was a piece of rock salt, since none of our food was ever salted. It was not supposed to taste good. We either had to sell something or steal to obtain a hunk of rock salt, even three or four ounces, and keep it with us. It became a treasure, like a piece of gold. Whenever we had a meal, we took out this rock salt and licked on it while sipping a spoonful of soup. There was a lot of thievery and we were forced to take extraordinary measures to protect this precious piece of salt. I had an old sock, which I was able to wash in cold water, and in this sock was my rock salt, carried inside of my belt at all times.

On rare occasions, the Russians looked for volunteers to go out and after ten hours of work unload hundred pound sacks of flour for the camp bakery. We all wanted to get in on these details because of the possibility of stealing a little bit of flour. We would tie our long underpants with a string and at the same time, our shirt sleeves. As we were working, hoisting these heavy bags which were far too heavy for us prisoners—for our bodies weighed little more than the sacks of flour themselves—once in a while we were able to poke a hole in the sacks and scoop the flour inside our pants and shirts. When we got back to the camp, we would get undressed, shake it out, and put a spoon or two into our morning and evening soup, making, we thought, virtually gourmet meals.

Soon, however, the Russian guards got wise to us, and before we returned to camp, they would untie our sleeves and the legs of our pants. All the flour would then fall onto the ground outside the camps. By the next morning it was gone. Probably some animals came around at night and ate the flour. So much for enhancing our meals.

One of the most perilous places in the camps was the latrine. It was a sixty-foot wooden beam over a trench about fifteen-feet deep. Prisoners would be sitting there thirty to forty at a time. Everybody had diarrhea or some kind of horrible intestinal problem. As terrible as it may sound, there were many occasions when prisoners were so sick, weak, or debilitated that they would fall backwards into the pit and nobody would pull them out. People became hardened and after a while such occurrences did not bother us any more. The Russians paid no attention, except that they wanted to know who fell in so they could put in their reports that another person had died.

As we discovered later, our situation in prison depended largely on what was going on back home. Any time the Russians thought the Communists had a chance of taking over in Austria or Germany, we were told we would be going home soon. The moment the election returns were in and the Communists had failed to make any headway in our homeland, however, we were back to square one. We were told it would be another five or ten years before we would be released, and of course, our morale would plummet.

In my years as a prisoner, I received three cards or letters from my parents. Neither did they receive mail from me. It was simply thrown away by the Russians. I understand that this violated the Geneva Convention, but the Russians didn't give a damn.

Christmas, 1945

The cold was intense. We huddled around a small wood-burning stove and the mood was somber for all of us. Not being home at Christmas was bad enough, but we knew nothing about the fate of our families. None of us knew whether we would ever see our families again, or if we would ever be able to leave Russia.

We would not, to be sure, if it were up to Comrade *Kapetan* Frankfurther, the NKVD captain who spoke German fluently and was filled with hatred for us. That was perhaps understandable after all his country went through, for the Russians had lost twenty million people in battling the German armed forces. Nevertheless, he was particularly bitter, and his behavior toward us was poisonous beyond that of any other Russian we encountered.

I remember how at about noon of our first Christmas Eve as prisoners, one of our fellow inmates came into the barracks, wet and snow-covered, with a large pine branch. How he got it none of us knew. We looked at one another and everyone began to cry. The past few months had been too much for us. We were determined to celebrate Christmas, though, so we nailed the pine branch to a bunk post, decorated it with bits of paper and sat down to look at our

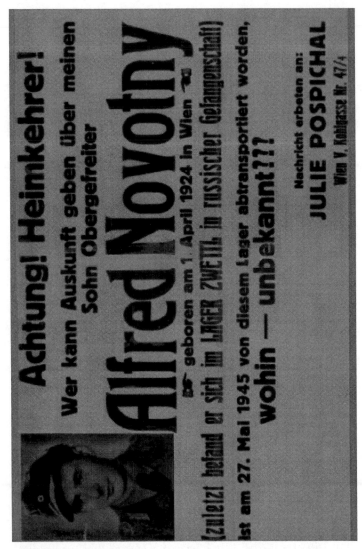

This poster was found by Novotny after returning from prison
camp in the USSR and arriving at Vienna's "Ostahnhof," or east
railroad station. The message reads, "Have you seen my son? MIA
since 27 May 1945." Novotny's mother made and posted this in
the hope that men arriving home from captivity would see it, and
perhaps remember encountering him in captivity.

"Christmas tree." We started to sing, *"Stille Nacht, Heilige Nacht"* when the door burst open. *Kapetan* Frankfurter stood there, arrogant, menacing, swaying. "Are you celebrating Christmas?" he asked, and we mutely nodded in unison.

"Not in Russia, you German pigs!" he shouted. Then he tore the branch off the bunkpost, opened the window, and threw it out into the snow.

"Don't ever try to celebrate any of your holidays again as long as you are in Russia," he said. Then he turned and left and we remained in our room, very hungry and very cold. Long into the night, we remained there and reminisced with one another about our past Christmases and what they had meant to us. This was one we would never forget, but it certainly was not a Christmas any of us would cherish.

The Enemy Within

The misery of Germans imprisoned by the Soviets during and after the war was only compounded by the lack of effective medical care. Many Allied prisoners experienced the same problem while in German camps during World War II. Nevertheless, this incident illuminates the inhumanity of Novotny's captors in ways that few other episodes can.

Fred Novotny remembers . . .

After being in prison in Soviet Georgia for about six months, something happened to me, and probably to many others. Whenever I ate the smallest amount of anything, I experienced a terrible pain in my stomach. It felt like a tornado was inside my body. I would seek help at the infirmary; every time I was told that nothing was wrong, that it was just a stomach ache. As time went on, I kept losing more and more weight and continued to complain to the doctor, to no avail.

One sip or bite of anything and the raging inside me began. After my release from captivity, at the hospital in Vienna, I repeatedly told the doctor. A follow-up examination finally produced results. To my great shock, I was told that I had a tapeworm in my bowels. "A what?" was my question. Treatments with drugs and garlic brought my sickness to a halt.

After five days of treatment, a thirty-foot-long tapeworm dropped out of my body, piece by piece. For over two years, this horrible creature had lived inside me, devouring everything I ate or drank. I am very sure that from teh outset, the Russian doctor knew what my sickness was. What a horrible, disgusting experience!

War Makes Strange Bedfellows . . .
My Estonian Friend

The Estonian nation suffered terribly from the 1940 Soviet occupation and the following war years. From a 1939 population of slightly over a million people, roughly 80,000 died by 1945. This was was equivalent to eight million deaths for the USA, based on its wartime population (the USA actually lost roughly 350,000 dead from the war). Tens of thousands of Estonians served willingly, or as conscripts, in the German military. Few had any love for Germany, but they desperately wanted to avoid a second Soviet occupation of their nation. Several thousand other Estonians (a handful as volunteers) served in the Red Army, and Novotny's friend would have been one of these.

Since attaining independence in 1991, Estonian historians have busily collected the accounts of the survivors of the war years. This is both to educate their people, and to provide instructional manuals for future generations, who are expected to have to face renewed Russian aggression.

Fred Novotny remembers . . .

One day at the *Lenin Schachti*, the coal mine, I saw a woman in a Soviet officer's uniform walking around our working areas, with her carbide lamp attached to her safety helmet, like the one I had on my head.

She said, "*Guten tag.*" I said, "*Sprechen sie Deutsch?*" Her answer was, "*Ja.*" She asked me how long I had been working down here. I asked her what she was doing 1,000

Pencil drawing of a bleak prison camp in Russia 1945. Artist:
Franz Eidenberger.

feet below ground. She simply left, but I could not help but
wonder how a woman in a Russian uniform could speak
such good German. A couple of days later I saw her again; in
German, she asked me, "Do you speak English?" I had
learned some English during my three years at the *"hotel
school"* in Vienna, even though my knowledge was more confined to grammar, with very little conversational English
experience. I said, yes, a little. She then asked me if could
teach her what I knew.

Since we were not to talk to Soviet citizens, I asked her if
either of us would get into trouble if found out. She told me
then that she was born an Estonian, was pressed into service
four years earlier, and because she was educated, advanced
to *leytenant*. However, the Russians did not trust non-
Russians. She ended up in the mines of Georgia as a liaison
officer (read: "prison guard").

As the days went on, we talked more and more. I knew
already how unhappy she was. She must have been between
twenty-five and thirty years old, not too glamorous, but
interesting to talk to. One day, she said, "Fredy (that was the

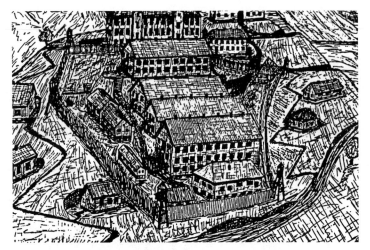

A crude sketch of the entrance to the camp. Artist Franz
Eidenberger.

name I told her), if you want to go home one of these days, it
is imperative that you learn Russian, and learn it well." It
would help me a lot, she said. "The more you know, the easier life will get for you! Mark my words!"

By now we had figured out how often we were alone in
the area during a week. As it turned out she was assigned to
my area of work on Tuesday, Wednesday, and Thursday. She
would bring in a little piece of paper on which she wrote five
Russian words in the German alphabet. The next day, I had
to recite those words, so every week I learned by heart at
least fifteen words—no grammar, just words. She said that
grammar would come later, after I learned many words.

I did the same with her and gave her five English words.
It was not long until she told me how well I was doing, and
that my Russian pronunciation was very good. Then she got
into grammar; soon I could put together entire spoken sentences. I felt good about this skill.

Soon the Russian guards found I could understand, so
they started using me to interpret, first simple things then

more and more. She followed up teaching me the Cyrillic alphabet, and I started reading pages in books, and so on.

Little advantages did follow, just as she predicted. Once in a while, I would get an apple or an onion from a guard for helping him to interpret. On a personal level, when you can communicate with people, pretty soon fear and prejudices are diminished and things become easier for everyone.

One day, my Estonian officer and teacher was gone. I was sad, because I had liked her. I never heard of her or saw her again. Such was life in a Russian prison. I often thought of her, wondering how things would have turned out for me if I would have not met her. Maybe these lines would have never been written!

Soviet Efficiency

Solzhenitsyn shares many accounts of this sort.

Fred Novotny remembers . . .

By 1946, I could speak Russian really well. I could read Cyrillic script and write in it as well. I always had a knack for languages, so I played interpreter on many occasions. One day, a guard summoned us together after we had spent a ten-hour day in the coal mines. He said we should eat but not go to sleep since we would be going out on another job. We protested loudly, but to no avail. It turned out the camp commandant had made a deal for money with a sawmill to have us move logs.

As we were marched to the sawmill, we prisoners agreed that we would act as if none of us understood any Russian. That way we would seem to not know what to do and simply wouldn't work. After we arrived, a Russian came over and told us, *"Vas mite trova!"* ("Move the logs to another location!"). We stood there like mules, not reacting at all. The guy got madder and madder, and he screamed over and over, *"Vas mite trova!"* Then the guard pointed at me and

Landscape drawing of Russia in 1945 by Fred Novotny.

said, "I think he understands." I had a small bout of craziness. He asked me how to say "take the wood" in German, and I replied, "*geht nach Hause.*" ("Go home").

He listened and then shouted, "*geht nach Hause.*" We slowly took our coats and walked away. He went nuts and I received a solid beating. We never worked that evening, though, despite my punishment. For once, we triumphed over our guards.

In 1946, as we found out later, the Red Cross delivered one blanket, one pair of shoes, and one sweater for every prisoner in the camp. We never saw any of it. The camp commander and his cronies sold everything on the black market and pocketed the money.

Major Grishtshenko, one of the commanders at the camp, had each of us bring back one brick hidden under our coats every day for a month. We had to steal them with the knowledge of the guards. We prisoners were forced to build a huge home above the camp for the major, all with the material we had stolen from the mines. Once the house was ready, a higher-ranking officer exposed the major to the NKVD and he disappeared, presumably to Siberia. The officer who had revealed the major's plot promptly moved into the new home we had built.

We also worked on apartment buildings for the populace, which were constructed in the most primitive fashion. Concrete was mixed on metal sheets by hand, slopped into buckets and carried across ten-inch wide boards as high as five floors up. It was highly dangerous work.

When the job was nearly finished, 120 toilet bowls were delivered, and to our amazement, all of them were diverted into the black market. The building was completed without toilets. Instead, it had holes in the floor with pipes sticking up. People moved in anyway, however. I asked the project supervisor (a prisoner himself, a Ukrainian who fought against the Russians under General Vlasov) how this was possible. He said people were desperate for shelter and would take anything. Six months later, he would request from Moscow another 120 new toilets, which would, six or eight months later, be installed. If caught, he said, he would be sent to Siberia where he would work as an engineer again, and do the same thing all over. Such was the chaos and disorder that afflicted post-war Russia.

The Russians' inefficiency became legendary. They dismantled entire factories in Germany and moved them by rail to Russia, where they would remain in boxcars for years and rot away because nobody knew how to put them together again.

Underground Passion

My existence as a prisoner was not completely without without pleasure, or something resembling it. It occurred 1,000 feet beneath the earth's surface in the *"Lenin Schachti,"* the Lenin coal mine in Tkvibuli, Georgia. There I met Tusia, a pharmacist from Moscow. She told me she was sent to the mines after having been found guilty of diverting medicine and drugs into the black market (the only way to make a living for most Soviet citizens). Her sentence was eight years at hard labor. She worked near me on the same level in the mine. I could not tell if she was pretty or not, because she was as filthy and completely covered with coal dust as I was.

By this time, in 1947, my Russian language skills were quite good, so we talked a lot. She wanted to know everything about life in western Europe. I kind of liked her, but I was afraid, however, to flirt with her because I had no way of knowing if she was a plant. Many people in the mines were there to spy and keep tabs on us.

One day during a ten-minute break, we were sitting on a large pile of coal. Suddenly, she leaned over and kissed me. One second later, our hands were all over each other's bodies. We were observed and reported; I was incarcerated for four days for fraternizing with a Soviet citizen. She was taken away, and I never could find out where she was taken.

It may seem amazing, but no matter how dismal life may be in war, or as a PW, when one is young, hormones don't stop working because of hardship or fear. That was life!

Life as a Miner

Work in the mines as a prisoner was extremely dangerous. We toiled in totally neglected, badly dilapidated mines that had not been used since 1919. Every day when we went down, we could never be sure that we would return from the depths. Accidents were numerous, and one could today count on one hand the days on which no one was injured or died. I don't know if there are any statistics on how many died in the mines.

In prison, more often than not, the Russians would appoint a prisoner to become leader in the camp. Very often this man would behave much more viciously than the Russian guards themselves. Self-preservation, not helping their comrades, was their common practice.

This little poem sticks with me!

"Hüte dich vor Sturm und Wind
und Deutsche die in Ausland sind!"
(Beware of storm and winds
and Germans in other countries!)

There was another little ditty which for many turned out to be true.

"Geniesse den Krieg,
der Friede wird Schrecklich sein."
(Enjoy the war, the peace will be horrible)

Unteroffizier Link

The prisoner appointed as our leader in our camp in Tkvibuli, Georgia, was a young sergeant named Link. He was a *Volksdeutsche* (an ethnic German), born in the Banat region in Romania. He spoke flawless Russian with a Ukrainian accent.

His job?—liaison between the Russian major who commanded the camp and the prisoners. As we found out over-time, he had the total trust of *Major* G., but not too much trust from the prisoners. He lived like a king: he had his own room and he profited from his involvement in every black market transaction. Anybody who wanted anything had to go through Link. The Russian *Major* led a charmed life. "Link will do it all," Link would joke with the commandant.

"One day you will wake up," he would say, "and I will be gone. What will you do without me!" The *Major* just laughed. One day Link was really gone. Six weeks later, he wrote to the *Major* from Germany and wished him the best. Later, he would tell fellow ex-prisoners in Germany he had had no problem posing as a Russian to get home.

Living Like a King

Early in 1947, during my days as a PW in Georgia, something happened in Austria that made the Russians believe that Austria might turn Red. The Communists won some parliamentary seats.

The Austrians in our camp, and other camps around the Soviet Union, were separated from the German prisoners.

For the first time in our almost two years of captivity, we received new shirts, trousers, and shoes. We were given extra food, to show us how "humane" the Russians were. We were then transported to Moscow, where they rerouted us to show off their pride and joy: the Moscow *Metro* (subway), "built all by slave labor." Spotlessly clean, with incredibly beautiful underground stations, it was basically the *only* thing they could and would show us.

We arrived in a city called Ivanovo-Vosnosensk, and were incarcerated in a camp that was cleaner and more livable than the old camp. The camp was called *"Umschlags Lager"* meaning, roughly, "A Camp for Change," meaning to change one's point of view. Simply put, this was a re-education camp where we were to be subjected to brainwashing designed to make us into compliant new Communists. Once our conversion was complete, we were to be released back to Austria to make sure Austria became and remained a Communist-dominated country.

For us, this was great; we all played along. We gladly incriminated ourselves by admitting all manner of past deeds, we "embraced" Marxist doctrine, and all the while lived better than we had in years. We did not work, and constantly thought to ourselves, "when I get home, to Hell with the Soviet Union!"

Our commissars even had us start a theater. The plays were all super-Soviet, but they were a great diversion for us. One such play was *"Panzerkreuzer* Potemkin," about the great Proletarian Communists and the evil Reactionary White Russians. I played a reactionary officer on the cruiser *Aurora* at the Leningrad harbor. What easy role playing! All I had to do was remember my lines and convincingly behave as if I detested Communists—and that took precious little acting!

On occasion, we were even taken out of the camp, and into Ivanovo, so sure were the Russians that they were creating a swarm of devout Communists. During one such outing, we were outside a *"gostinitsa"* (tavern). A very nice man, wearing a coat, tie, and a hat, came out with a young boy. He started a conversation with me, very scared that someone

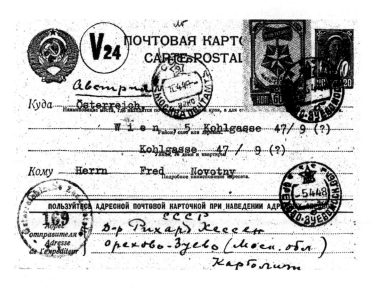

Letters Novotny received in Vienna after returning home, sent by those still in the Soviet Union. The top one was sent Karl Otto, from his prison camp. The one below came from I.G. Farben engineer Herbert Stauffer.

might listen in. We hit it off right away and talked for about one hour.

As it turned out, his name was *Diplom-Ingenieur (certified engineer)* Herbert Stauffer, and he used to be one of the higher ups at I.G. Farben, the giant enterprise. It was one of the big companies of the German war industry, he said.

He and his family were awakened during the night, as were many other families, allowed only the clothing on their backs, and after a four-week journey, ended up at Ivanovo. Trains loaded with the dismantled I.G. Farben factory at which he had worked followed.

He asked me, if I should make it home, if I would please write to him when I got there. He also asked if I could send him some stamps for his son's collection. It took me one more year to get home. I tried the address he gave me a year earlier, and miraculously, six months later I got the first answer. It was not a pretty picture. The family had no knowledge of Russian, the son was in a Russian school, and the father worked as an engineer. The family was very unhappy, knowing they might never return.

I.G. Farben engineer Herbert Stauffer sent Fred Novotny this photo from the Soviet Union during 1949. At left is Herbert's son, sixteen year-old Horst.

We corresponded for four years. I could read their frustrations and fears between the lines. Then we lost contact. Twenty years later, I started inquiring in Germany, only to find that they were still not home. What happened to them happened to tens of thousands of other families.

The Communists did not win in Austria. When the Russians realized this, we were treated the old way again, but for four months life had been easier.

The Georgians

The Georgian experience was similar to that of the Estonians, though the Georgians spent longer under the Communist yoke. Thousands of Georgian PWs aided the Germans during the war, and those that were recaptured often received the harshest treatment of anyone in the Gulag.

Fred Novotny remembers . . .

During my years in the coal mines I met many Georgians, a very articulate, often restless, people, fiercely proud of their heritage. Totally opposed to Communism, they never let on to any Russians that they felt that way...but the moment they were out of earshot of Russians they would let loose, verbally attacking the regime and its leaders. They often insisted that the day would come when they would be free again, and that then the Russians would pay for what they had done (See Chechnya today!).

We were told by German soldiers who fought Georgian units that they were fierce fighters. In prison, however, they fraternized with us at any occasion, saying often that they wished we Germans had won. I still remember a few Georgian words or phrases I learned: *Momezi Bury* (Give me bread). *Erti, Uri, Sami* (one, two, three), and so on. I also learned how to write my name in Georgian. They really were quite familiar with us in the camps.

New Soviet Citizens

Some of the victims of this project, along with previously mentioned factory workers, and members of the Volga German community, were able to emigrate to Germany during the 1990s, after the breakup of the USSR. Most vanished from recorded history.

Fred Novotny remembers . . .

Here is a story, very little known, that may have affected more than 100,000 German soldiers, men and women, from 1947 on.

In early 1947, something strange and exciting happened in the prison camps across the Soviet Union. German female prisoners were integrated into the camps. Subsequently, nature started to take its course. Girls became pregnant, and that is when a diabolical Soviet scheme started to emerge.

Pregnant females would be interrogated, the man in their lives would be found out, and so it went: both would be brought to special interrogators, and outwardly friendly conversations ensued.

The Russian officer would start, "What a happy occasion, after this horrible war, which took so many lives. Now, you would not want an innocent child to be born behind barbed wire! Let us show you that the Soviet Union, which you so much feared, is very humane. Let us suggest the following to you: Here, you sign a statement that you are the parents of this child to be born. With this in hand, we will arrange an apartment for you outside the camp. It will have kitchen facilities, and so on, so that for the first month of the child's life, you are practically free and the child grows up normally until you both are released to go home."

What the Soviets failed to mention was that the moment the parents were out of the camp, they were no longer under the auspices of the Geneva Convention. They would be taken off the roster of the prison camp. Since the child was born outside the camp, he or she was, in fact, a Soviet citizen. With the child a Soviet citizen, and the parents for all practical purposes no longer PWs, tens of thousands of such new Soviet families could be transferred to remote areas in Siberia where they subsequently helped to establish new communities. The Germans, with their skills and know-how, would in this way actively cultivate and build new areas in the Soviet Union.

The fact that their new Soviet citizens were now outside any international control meant really very little anyway, since the Soviets never cared about international rules anyway. As we knew ourselves, hundreds of thousands of packages from home or the International Red Cross that were sent our way in prison were never given to us, but diverted to the black market to line Socialist pockets. In all my time in prison, I never saw a package, or designated Red Cross supplies (socks, sweaters, and so on) at all.

After nearly fifty years, during the Gorbachev era, some of those now-Russian families trickled back to their former roots, and perhaps were finally reunited with living relatives. This is one of the sad stories little known or written about even to this day!

4

Freedom and Capitalism

Coming Home?

This was a case where Novotny was fortunate to be Austrian. The hope that Austria would turn Communist remained, which improved that country's relations with the USSR. Most Germans were not released from Soviet captivity until 1949 at the earliest. Certain "hardcore cases," such as Waffen-SS *men, only received their release due to Adenauer's personal intervention, returning home as late as January 1956. Several Western European* Waffen-SS *men were held longer, including four Dutch volunteers who only returned to the Netherlands during 1962!*

Luftwaffe Major Erich Hartmann was credited with 352 aerial "kills" during the war, by far the most in history. He had many more that were not recognized, as did all leading aces in every country. Hartmann was considered a prize prisoner, and was not released until 1955.

Fred Novotny remembers . . .

On the last day in December 1947, we were issued new uniforms, new underwear, and new shoes, and were told it was time to go home. We did not believe it. We had been disappointed so many times before and there was no display of joy at all until we actually were marched onto a train and were rolling west.

It was a reprise of our horrible journey to the east, but this time we were going in the right direction. Our journey home

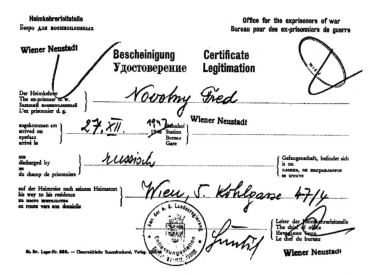

Novotny's release papers, indicating to Allied officials that as of 27 December 1947, he was on his way home to Vienna.

took about two-and-a-half weeks, and it was the end of 1947. Then, at the Hungarian border, we were held up for twenty-four hours. We began to be afraid they were going to turn the train around and take us back into Russia, but the next morning, we actually rolled across the Hungarian-Austrian border and slowly creaked toward the east railroad station, or *Ostbahnhof*, in Vienna. My parents, who had scanned the newspapers daily for news of arriving prisoners, somehow knew that I was arriving.

As we got off the train, there were my two sisters, my father, and my mother. We were speechless. After so many years of not seeing one another, not knowing what had happened, being reunited was indescribable. The emotions, the happiness, the relief were all wonderful beyond words. We had nothing to say. We simply held onto one another for a long time.

Finally, my mother explained that things would look somewhat different when we got home since our apartment had been bombed and she had to move into smaller quarters.

It did not matter. We had survived this most terrible war in history and that was all that mattered.

Once we had settled down, I spent several days dashing from one office to the next, trying to prove who I was. The Russians had taken all our papers in 1945 and never returned anything to us.

Then came the thanks from the Fatherland. There was nothing like the GI Bill for us. No free college, no bonus, no monthly check. I thought of the many years that were taken from us, the youth that I never really had. Still, I was thankful to be back home. I was thankful to be alive.

Living in the USA for 46 years, I sometimes watch with amazement on TV or read about what America did and is doing for its homecoming fighting men. The GI Bill, assistance in locating jobs, community help, medical and psychiatric care, counseling, vocational training, and on and on.

Our thanks from Germany?

1. Two free streetcar tickets, worth ten cents each, to be able to report to certain authorities.
2. Two packages of cigarettes, worth fifteen cents each.
3. Find your own job!
4. Help yourself or no one will.
5. Never mind if things are not right in your head, don't bother the doctors! Work it out yourself!

As the Gallic general, Brennus, said to the Romans in 390 B.C.: *Vae victis!* ("Woe to the vanquished!")

I thought of a saying from another prisoner of the Russians. This was written by *Major* Erich Hartmann, the greatest combat fighter pilot of all time, who was imprisoned in the Soviet Union for ten years, from 1945 until 1955. "Only those who have endured Soviet imprisonment are entitled to valid opinions concerning it," he wrote. I will say no more.

Back home, the days went by. Mama was told by our doctors not to give me any solid food—mainly liquids and mostly diet food—because of many years of having nothing substantial at all. A premature return to normal food could have been completely disruptive to my system. As we found out later, many returning prisoners paid no attention to such warnings, and died because their stomachs could not handle the sudden ingestion of rich, solid sustenance. After having endured the horrors of all those years in prison, they would die from trying to readjust too quickly to life back in Germany or Austria.

Then, after six months, I was ready to go back to work to the place where I had been an apprentice, and I was given a job as a waiter. While I enjoyed my work, there was little good food and the menus were extremely limited. Still, after all the gray, miserable war years, people were anxious to go out again, especially on weekends. I quickly got back into the flow of the business I had left seven years earlier.

In 1949, I met a young girl who I immediately liked and with whom I fell in love. Her name was Elizabeth Telecky. We were married on 27 August 1951, and are still married to this day. We have a wonderful daughter, Eva, who lives in

Fred and Lisl's wedding photo, 1951.

Toronto, and two grandchildren, Michelle and Claudia, whose hard-working father owns a manufacturing company in Toronto. And so it went.

Lisl

My wife, Lisl—Austrian for Elizabeth—had her own stories about the war and the years afterwards. She was only four- teen when the war ended and she lived with her parents and her brother, Robert, in the Austrian resort town of Baden, south of Vienna.

Food was very scarce during the war and children often went to nearby farms to gather a few potatoes. Her mother would take day-long train trips into the country to her rela- tives and come back with a half-dozen eggs and a couple of pounds of meat.

When the war ended, the Russians made Baden their headquarters in Austria, and there were horrible reports of

A portrait of Elizabeth
Novotny, circa 1947
when she was sixteen.

plundering and rape. The Russians requisitioned all but one room from my wife's family and remained there for years.

When they first arrived, the people were terrified. Her father took his wife and the children into a deep wooded area above the town. While it sounds funny now, people do strange things when caught in such panic situations—he carried a rucksack, supposedly filled with necessary supplies, but when he opened it in the woods, he discovered he had packed silk pajamas, slippers and a toothbrush. All the things they really needed had been left behind.

After three days with no food or water, they returned to their house, which the Russians had not as yet found. There were rumors everywhere, though, about the wholesale rape of females from ten-year-old girls to grandmothers.

Lisl was hidden by her parents in a recess in the wall, over which a large wardrobe was pushed. She was given a large knife. If the Russians had found her, there is no telling what they might have done. The Russians who eventually moved into the house, however, were officers, who were much better behaved than the regular troops. Lisl was able to come out, but to this day, she speaks of those fearful times hidden behind the wardrobe.

The Spy Who Would Not Be

After a few months of recuperating and getting back some of my strength, I went back to work at the place I had to leave to to help build the Thousand-Year Reich . . . and also to save Germany from the *Untermenschen*. History worked out in reverse.

One day, I was working at the outdoor terrace of the Kahlenberg Restaurant, overlooking my beloved Vienna. Four Russian officers were seated at my station. All, as I observed, were well-dressed and well-groomed, contrary to what I was accustomed to during the war. I could hear them speaking English, German, and Russian. I approached their table and spoke German to them, not letting on that I could understand and speak Russian.

One young officer—he called himself Peter—looked very western. He spoke perfect German. He talked to me and laughed when I told them I had the privilege of tasting their food in Russia. When they left, they told me how great my recommendations were, and how fine the food and service had been. They left a very large tip.

A few days later, the officer named Peter was seated at my station again. He told me that he had asked for me because he enjoyed our conversation during his previous visit. After he had finished lunch, he engaged in small talk, asking about the life of the people in Austria with so much destruction from the war.

Within a few weeks, he became a regular guest of mine, and I kind of liked him. He was well educated, worldly, kind, and witty. Soon our conversations became more private. He told me that he often went to Switzerland, which I found rather odd, since that was a neutral country, but I thought nothing of it. One day he asked if I would lunch with him on my day off. So I did. We went to a downtown restaurant, ate, drank, and had a good time. I still never spoke to him in Russian.

He told me that day that he trusted me and said that he was planning to defect to Switzerland. He said he had a friend there and might need one in Austria for assistance when the time of his flight came.

I discovered later that this was part of an elaborate plot to gain my confidence and set me up for things to come.

After one of our meetings, he asked how much money I made. I told him, and he said that since I was a smart young man, I could make several times that. As part of the occupation troops in Europe, he said, he was paid very well, and if I wanted a free vacation, he would take care of it as a gesture of friendship. We talked about many things and then he pushed an envelope across the desk. Inside was $1,000 in American currency. This translated to 25,000 Austrian schillings (I made 1,500 schillings a month at the time.)

Suddenly, a light went on in my head. I was confused and frightened. He wanted me to spy for the Russians. I wondered if I was already involved. He suggested I go to Salzburg, take the camera he offered me, and take a few pictures of American troops, tanks, or anything else I might see since, saying, "they like to be photographed."

I looked at him and asked how I could ever trust him again since the reason for all this friendship was to recruit me as a spy. I told him I had had enough of war and prison for a lifetime.

He said to me he was in big trouble since he had informed his superiors I already was on their side. He was so sure, he said, and now he didn't know what would happen to him.

I gave him back the money, feeling enormous relief that I had declined his offer.

I felt so stupid, though. How had I not seen this coming. And what now? Would they follow me around? I confided this to my father and he said I should tell the Americans.

I did. I described Peter and his associates. The Americans told me not to let the Russians know I had talked to them, but to go on with the meetings and then report to them.

My reply was the same: Thanks, but no thanks. I wanted nothing to do with spying, for either side.

I never saw Peter again. They probably pulled him out of Vienna. How easily I could have been entangled in the Cold War spy games. I am glad I was able to walk away in one piece.

To the USA

In 1952, my Uncle Otto, who lived in Springfield, Illinois, came with my Aunt Mimi to visit Vienna. During his stay, he talked to me about the possibility of emigrating to the United States to try to make a life for myself and my family. It sounded wonderful, and I couldn't imagine living in a country where everything seemed to be so plentiful, so free, so distant from the war and its memories.

My sister, Jutta, was also intrigued. Uncle Otto sponsored her, and so she came to the United States during 1955. The next year, Jan Galba, her friend from Vienna, joined her in Springfield.

I took out a visa application of my own to come to the United States and it finally came through in 1956. By that time, some of the wounds of World War II had healed. We had made a lot of progress. I had an excellent job, made good money, and we had a modest apartment, nicely furnished with a lot of the accessories many people did not yet have. It was a difficult decision whether to go to the United States or to stay where we were for by 1950, I had developed a very good reputation in our industry. By that time, working at the Kahlenberg, I had received a rare offer to work at one of Austria's finest and most prestigious hotels, the Hotel Sacher. It has been known for years for its famous "Sacher *Torte*" and for the uncompromising service and quality of food. I accepted the offer and found taht I fit in there very quickly. In the course of my duties, I became acquainted with many ambassadors and heads of state from around the world, since this hotel was a meeting place for diplomats and aristocrats, for the rich and the famous. I am proud to have worked there.

My beautiful young wife and I had to make some agonizing decisions. We also had a lovely daughter, Eva, born in 1955, and this weighed heavily upon us. How would we manage, leaving everything behind, our parents, everybody we knew and loved?

Finally, after days and nights of discussing this, we decided that I would go to America for six months and see whether we could make a living there and have a better chance for advancement and success than in Austria. At that time, like almost any place in Europe, it might take a long time for a young person to achieve real success. Unlike America, if you had a good job, you didn't leave it.

We also had to decide what to do with all the material goods we had acquired. It finally came down to the determination that no matter how new or expensive, we had to practically give everything away because no one wanted to pay anything, or had the money to pay anyway. Here I was, with

Fred arriving in New York on 26 March 1956. After a brief layover, it was on to Chicago and a new epoch in the author's life.

the last five years of earnings practically going down the drain, all to roll the dice on going to America.

If we decided I would stay in America and she would join me, we had to dispose of the apartment and sell everything or give it away. It was most difficult for her. At the time, I still had a mother and father in Austria, and my wife had only her mother left. Her only brother lived in Brazil and hadn't been home in years. Her mother would be completely alone.

On 26 March 1956, I climbed aboard a TWA Lockheed Constellation bound from Vienna to New York, then flew on to Chicago's Midway Airport, where my mother's sister and her husband picked me up.

I remember very little about the car trip from Chicago to Springfield, except for the vast spaces, which reminded me, in their vastness, of Russia. My relatives had a nice house on Illinois Street and while I could have stayed there rent-free, I didn't want to take advantage of anybody. I got a job at what was then the best hotel in Springfield, the Leland. Since I had no money, I walked the fifteen blocks to work and back home. I worked as a *sommelier*, or wine steward.

My boss, Jim Bollinger, took me aside on the second day of my job and told me, "Mr. Novotny, I know you just came from Europe, I know you spent many years in a Russian prison camp, and I want you to know something. You will see here a tremendous waste of food and material and I want to apologize in advance since you know what the rest of the world's living conditions are. There is nothing we can do. That is just the way we live. We are a very rich country and you have to be tolerant when you see things like this."

It was true, too. It was fantastic, the amount of meat and vegetables and rolls and butter that were thrown out every evening. It wasn't controlled the way it had been in Europe. I am glad Mr. Bollinger told me about it in advance, as it was fairly shocking to me.

I should add here that I didn't have bad feelings toward America and Americans. As angry as my comrades and I were at the Americans in May 1945, feeling horribly betrayed, time heals all wounds. The time in Russian prison, with all its bad days; the many positive things Americans did for Germany and Austria; the help we got from my American cousin after the war—all these things helped overcome the bad feelings of 1945. After all, when I left for America, eleven years had passed since the end of the war.

But Will It Play in Peoria?

A short time later, through my cousin's husband, I met a Swiss gentleman named Ferd Sperl, who was general manager of the Hotel Pere Marquette in Peoria. I had never heard of Peoria before and had no idea what kind of town it was. My cousin, however, came to Peoria with me and introduced me to Mr. Sperl, who, being Swiss-born, spoke excellent German. It made me feel comfortable, and I accepted a job with him on 1 July 1956.

When I arrived in Peoria, an "office" was all ready for me. It was a cubbyhole down in the basement next to a noisy bottle chute. Understandably, I was discouraged, but I had to give it my best. I had Elizabeth and the baby back in Vienna, and I had to make it. Even the salary was low, however, compared to what I had been making in Vienna as a headwaiter.

Here, at the Pere Marquette in Peoria, though, communication was very difficult for me. I was in charge of sixteen bartenders, and when Mr. Sperl asked me what I knew about the business, I told him honestly, and that seemed to be sufficient. When you come from Europe, you know what things ought to be done, but you do not always know quite *how* to do them in America. I had to learn a lot about the business end. Since I spoke very little English—mainly waiter's English—it was a real problem. I carried a small dictionary in my pocket and when a bartender would ask me something— maybe a question containing five or six words—I understood three, and I tried to remember one or two I didn't understand. I would say, "just a moment" and then disappear someplace and open my little book to find the word, and then go back and say "yes" or "no," or "do" or "do not." That is how I got my feet wet, very slowly and with great difficulty, in the United States.

To save money, I lived at the YMCA. It was very inexpensive. A few dollars per week went to my lodging, and I saved every penny of the rest of what I made. On 6 October 1956, Elizabeth and our fourteen-month-old baby, Eva, arrived in the States. Three days previously, Jutta had married Jan in Springfield. By then, I had rented a small house on a nice street in Peoria and I had purchased a red 1953 Pontiac. It was a fine car, which by today's standards looked like a tank. It also was built like a tank. I had bought all new furniture, even a small television set, on credit, with the help of my uncle. I wanted my wife to come in and find her life a little easier by having certain essentials in place in our home. It helped immensely.

After the wonderful joy of our reunion, however, the hard times started. My wife was discouraged and depressed. She

had left behind her widowed mother. She was an independent young woman before, but now she needed me for
everything—shopping, reading, television, answering the
phone, everything one needs to get by in a strange, foreign
country. It was very hard, especially because I was learning a
new job and my head was filled with a thousand things I had
to remember.

It was increasingly difficult for Elizabeth. When the phone
rang, for instance, she would not pick it up. She did not
know what to say. She would not understand what the person on the other end was saying, and she could not easily
make friends with the neighbors, since she could not talk
with them. They thought maybe we were snobs and they
avoided us. Eventually, though, everything worked out for
the best. Still, day after day, we would look at each other and
we both knew we wanted to go back home to Vienna. I was
discouraged with my work. I had never worked in conditions like this before. Money was very tight. There was barely enough to buy groceries. My sister moved from
Springfield to Peoria with her husband and that helped, but
they also were struggling. Sometimes we had to borrow ten
dollars or so to pay for our groceries.

So, going back was always on our minds, but so was our
pride. We didn't want to admit that we had failed, that we
couldn't hack it. The will to succeed took over. It took nearly
three years, and it is hard to explain how many things went
wrong and kept us down and depressed during those years.

Slowly, though, we became adjusted to life in America.
Life became easier. I became, after two and a half years, manager of a small motel which, fortunately, prospered after I
took it over; my experience began to tell. I finally stated to
make acquaintances. We found a lot of other Europeans,
mainly Germans and Swiss, who arrived here and suffered
the same handicaps as we experienced. We discovered an
area called Hickory Grove, which was a hangout for dis-
placed Europeans. We ate food that gave us a feel of our
homeland. We had very little, but on Sundays, we would
play soccer, sing together, and we began to feel more at home
in this new country of ours.

One evening a week, I was able to have my extended family in for dinner. This turned out to be very important time, and we still do the same. Now, my daughter living in Canada, does the same with her husband. It is vital to have a very nice night together once a week to discuss problems and enjoy each other's company.

The days eventually came when our parents inevitably became older and infirm, and we were far away. First, my Mama died, and I had to rush home. I had no money, though, so I had to borrow it for my airplane ticket. I had to go. I could always make the money again. The same thing happened when my wife's mother died and when my Papa died. When Elizabeth's brother died in Brazil at the age of fifty-two, we had lost all of our closest family members. Losing one's family is very hard in whatever circumstances, and after World War II, in particular, families were often scattered all over the globe.

In 1964, I became a partner in what used to be called the Voyager Inn in Peoria, the city's first luxury motel. It was a highly successful 180-room motel/hotel in downtown Peoria and I remained there for fourteen years. Afterward, I left and went to Chicago in 1970 to help build a hotel, which later was named Nordic Hills.

In 1971, I had an opportunity to work with a man I had known for the previous ten years. He was Phil Hauter, who liked me, the way I worked, and what I did for business. He proposed that we should get together and I should come up with a business concept. We decided on a place out in the cornfields of Morton, Illinois, about ten miles from Peoria. It was to be called the Peppermill.

Other partners were brought in, among them Congressman Robert Michel; his wife, Corrine; and Hauter's daughter and son-in-law.

We worked very hard. I was there virtually all the time. The place became one of the most successful restaurants in all of Illinois. I had many articles written about my part in the venture in business magazines and in food reviews.

During that time, too, I participated in many food and beverage competitions. Luckily, I won many top prizes in the

United States and earned a very good name in the midwest in our industry.

Things were going very well. We bought a new home in 1967 and we still own it. It is located at the edge of the Forest Park Nature Center just north of Peoria, and we have always loved being close to nature. It is not quite like the Vienna Woods, but my wife and I have become ardent hikers and can be found almost every day for at least an hour during six or seven months of the year, doing our hiking and staying fit.

Many funny things happened to us in the process of becoming Americans, as they do to almost any immigrants to a strange country. I once asked my wife why the neighbors were not at home because I did not see any lights on at their house. She said they had told her they were going to see the rabbits. I asked her why they would want to go to look at rabbits, and we talked about this. We were mystified about the difference between Cedar Rapids and other types of rabbits.

Another time we were at a concert at Glen Oak Park in Peoria with my sister. On the way out, she asked if we could meet on Wednesday, and we said we could, at about six o'clock. Six in German is spelled "*sechs*" and my wife shouted across the street, "*Sechs* is fine." Some elderly ladies stopped to look at us and shook their heads. This definitely "did not play" in Peoria!

My brother-in-law, who is from Czechoslovakia, had learned a little English in a class. He had learned the word "go" for walking. The first few times he came to an intersection where the light turned green, he did not walk, because he did not see the word "go." He stood there through three or four changes until he finally followed the people.

I had always wanted to speak English well, but the hardest letter for people not born in America is the letter "w." In German, it is always pronounced like an English "v." For a long time, instead of "veal cutlets," I would think, "wheel cutlet" just to get the sound right in my German-speaking brain.

We also found ourselves increasingly assimilated into the culture of America. While we were here, we would dream of everything in Austria being perfect, the mountains, the music, the scenery, the culture. We would get very upset if anyone said a bad word about Austria; when we went to visit in Europe, however, we would react in the same way about America. Anytime anybody said anything bad about America, we would defend our new country in the same way we defended Austria.

We became finally very accepted in the city of Peoria. Many, many people knew us. We had, and still have, many acquaintances and friends.

In 1973, I became president of the Illinois Hotel Association. I had to make an acceptance speech and I worried for days about it. I didn't want to sound corny, or like a hick, so I wrote what I thought was a brilliant speech. The moment I stood up at the podium before a couple of hundred high-powered hotel executives, however, my knees started to shake and I could not read a single word. I bowed and began ad-libbing. I said what I wanted to say and even received a good deal of applause. It was like a nightmare for me, though, that first important speech, but everybody learns and it becomes a lot easier. Or does it?

Over the years, I took a lot of young people under my care and taught them how to succeed in business. Even today, when I walk the streets downtown, people who used to work with me will come up and thank me. It is a great feeling.

Unfortunately, in 1976, my great friend and partner, Mr. Phil Hauter, passed away. Due to some contractual problems, I would have been forced to cooperate with several people with whom I simply could not work. So I sold my shares of the Peppermill, the place I had built from scratch and which had become so successful and famous in Central Illinois. It was a very depressing time. I did some restaurant consulting for about a year, and did well, but it was not what I wanted to do.

Then I met a man in Peoria who had a very successful hotel and food business. I had known him for some time. He was James Jumer of Jumer Hotels, and he approached me and offered me a job helping him manage his hotels. It was a new, interesting challenge for me. I liked working with

Jumer and I liked his concept of the old world inn transplanted into Illinois and Iowa with their baroque, Germanic furnishings and their continental food.

In 1989, I turned sixty-five. By then, my experience in the hotel and food business went back more than fifty years, and I thought I should take it a little easier. I semi-retired from the company. That same year, I was honored by the Hotel Association as Hotelier of the Year, with a party in Chicago and subsequently at the Peoria Civic Center—it was a great way to leave a business I loved.

Now, as I write this book, I have been in the same business for fifty-seven years. I have written a small book about drinks and unique sandwiches which had a successful sales run, and now I mainly want to be with my family. My daughter lives in Toronto with our two grandchildren, Michelle and Claudia, and we spend as much time as possible with them. This will let them know where we came from, how we ended up in the United States, and why they were born here. It has been a long, long journey and I am thankful it has brought us here.

Looking back after nearly sixty years, this period of my life and history, with all its horrors, and also its amusing moments and satisfying results, made me mentally and emotionally stronger. I no longer carry any grudges toward whoever made me lose what might have been the best years of my life, from age seventeen to age twenty-four.

I am happy. I am content. I have a great, loving family. I am at an age now where I take one day at a time. The only change in my thinking is, "I don't buy any green bananas anymore," to quote the great former congressman Claude Pepper.

I am privileged to have had the opportunity to tell this story, not only to my daughter and two granddaughters, but to all the people whose lives were touched and changed forever because of what my generation experienced. If stories such as mine are not told now, they will probably be lost forever.

In reflective moments, I still wonder how it all happened, this terrible war, this orgy of killing. We were politicized practically from birth; we were so bombarded with skillfully conceived propaganda that we actually *believed* in the myths in which we were immersed. Even when our fathers told us differently, we were convinced that we were defending our nation against the world, that we would win the war, and that the *Reich* for which we were bleeding and dying would endure for a thousand years. Instead, just seven years after the *Anschluss*, beaten, lost, and downtrodden, we were consigned to waste away in prison camps, in far-away cities with the strangest of names. How could they do it? How could young minds be so manipulated? How could *we* do it? Has the world learned from it sixty years later?

My answer is NO.

———⟫●⟪———

Even now, despite all my good fortune in America, and despite all the time that has passed, there are things I can never forget. Sometimes, in the stillness and safety of my own house, the rattle of gunfire, the whine and crack of bullets, the thumping and crashing of artillery and rockets, and the grinding roar of tanks echo in my ears. The anguish of endless days at the prison camp, wondering if I would ever be freed, still rudely intrudes on the most placid of moments. The momentary experience in the foxhole with Walter Grube leaps to the forefront of my mind on occasions that are sometimes too many for my comfort, and too few for my conscience. Finally, the face of the young Russian soldier on the other side of the street drifts into my memory's gaze, and I think about that long, long moment we shared until we both turned away and, for once, chose mercy and life amidst the mayhem of war.

I will never know, but I hope his life has turned out as well as mine.